Lernkrimi Englisch

Bullets over Bristol

Gina Billy
Jennifer Pickett

Weitere Informationen zu Compact Lernkrimis finden Sie am Ende des Buches und unter www.lernkrimi.de.

© Compact Verlag GmbH
Baierbrunner Straße 27, 81379 München
Ausgabe 2015
3. Auflage

Alle Rechte vorbehalten. Nachdruck, auch auszugsweise,
nur mit ausdrücklicher Genehmigung des Verlages gestattet.

Chefredaktion: Dr. Matthias Feldbaum
Redaktion: Christiane Grosskopf, Helga Aichele
Fachredaktion: Nathalie Russell
Produktion: Ute Hausleiter
Titelillustration: Karl Knospe
Lernkrimi-Logo: Carsten Abelbeck
Gestaltung: EKH Werbeagentur GbR, textum GmbH
Umschlaggestaltung: EKH Werbeagentur GbR, Hartmut Baier

ISBN 978-3-8174-8544-4
381748544/3

www.compactverlag.de, www.lernkrimi.de

Vorwort

Liebe Leserin, lieber Leser,

sicher zum Lernerfolg – mit Spaß und Spannung! Die Compact Lernkrimis mit ihrer Kombination aus Lektüre und didaktischem Übungsanteil eignen sich hervorragend, um breite Sprachkompetenzen in der Fremdsprache zu erwerben. Der Lerner wird dabei durch die spannende Handlung, das angemessene Sprachniveau und den stetig ansteigenden Schwierigkeitsgrad der Übungen gefördert und motiviert.
Entwickelt nach neuesten Erkenntnissen der Fremdsprachendidaktik, sind Compact Lernkrimis das ideale Medium für einen Lernerfolg im Selbststudium. Durch die kleinen Texteinheiten und den hohen Übungsanteil sind sie aber auch als Unterrichtslektüre bestens geeignet.

So lernen Sie mit Compact Lernkrimis:
- **Mit Begeisterung lernen:** Die packende Krimihandlung motiviert Sie beim Lesen des englischen Originaltextes.
- **Wissen intensivieren und erweitern:** Durch die Kombination aus didaktisierter Lektüre und textbezogenen Übungen testen und trainieren Sie Ihre Sprachkenntnisse effektiv. Vokabelangaben auf jeder Seite unterstützen Sie beim Lesen.
- **Systematisch lernen:** Knüpfen Sie an Ihr individuelles Sprachniveau an und setzen Sie eigene Lernziele – linear im Schwierigkeitsgrad ansteigend oder mit punktuellen Schwerpunkten von Grundwortschatz bis Hörverstehen.
- **Unabhängig sein:** Lernen Sie ganz individuell – wo und wann Sie wollen.

Viel Spaß beim **spannend Englisch lernen**
wünscht Ihnen

Prof. Dr. Christiane Neveling
Didaktik der romanischen Sprachen, Universität Leipzig

Inhalt

Bullets over Bristol 5

The Spy's Last Shot 41

Waving Death 79

Final Test 122

Answers 131

Glossary 138

List of Exercises 153

Die Ereignisse und die handelnden Personen in diesem Buch sind frei erfunden. Etwaige Ähnlichkeiten mit tatsächlichen Ereignissen oder lebenden Personen wären rein zufällig und unbeabsichtigt.

Bullets over Bristol

Jennifer Pickett

Murder

Stephen **slipped** silently into the house. His heart was **thumping** violently in his chest. He made his way up the darkened stairs to his room. With every step he was terrified that he would be caught. He lay fully clothed on his bed, his body **tense** and his eyes moving wildly around the room. He was exhausted but sleep wouldn't come. The hours **crawled** slowly past.

"Dead, dead, dead."

The word **pounded relentlessly** in his mind. From downstairs he could hear the voices of his mother and stepfather talking as they made breakfast. His mother's quiet voice was soon lost under the louder, more aggressive voice of Arthur, his step-dad. He was complaining about the traffic on the Clifton **Suspension Bridge**. Stephen buried his head under his pillow.

"What am I going to do?"

He bit his lip to stop himself from crying out in fear. He had never been so scared in his life. Every time he shut his eyes he could see the whole horrible scene playing out in front of him. He knew it was only a question of time before the police caught up with him.

to slip	*hier:* hineinschleichen
to thump	*hier:* pochen
tense	angespannt
to crawl	kriechen
to pound	hämmern
relentlessly	schonungslos
suspension bridge	Hängebrücke

Detective Inspector Charles Billington and Sergeant Daniel Fox looked at the busy area in front of them. DI Billington rubbed his hands over his tired face. Stubble prickled against his skin where he hadn't shaved that morning. He had put on fresh clothes that morning but they already looked creased. At forty-five he was getting too old for these early mornings.

> **Exercise 1: Adjectives.** Lesen Sie weiter und unterstreichen Sie alle sieben Adjektive!
>
> His young sergeant, however, looked rested and seemed full of energy. Danny's thick black hair was slightly messy, but other than that he looked as if he had just come from a relaxing afternoon watching the cricket!

The usual peace of these woods on the hills over Bristol had been disturbed. The area was now alive with activity. The black and yellow police tape fluttered in the breeze. Even though it was still early, a small crowd had gathered. Detective Inspector Billington sighed as he recognized the reporter from the local newspaper. The serious-looking constable on duty was doing a good job of making sure that no one crossed the tape into the crime scene behind, but the detective knew it wouldn't be long before the questions started.

"Right, Danny, let's get this over with."

He led his sergeant past the constable at the tape and into the clearing in the centre of the woods. He nodded at the forensics team at work.

stubble	Bartstoppeln
creased	zerknittert
to disturb	stören
to sigh	seufzen
crime scene	Tatort
⚡ to get sth. over with	etw. hinter sich bringen
clearing	Lichtung
forensics	Kriminaltechnik

"Morning, Andrew, what have you got for me, then?"
Andrew Cavendish, the forensics team leader sat back on his heels and looked up at him.
"The body is of a man about fifty years old. Cause of death is likely to be a shotgun blast to the chest."

The body was lying on its back with its arms out to the sides. The man was obviously dead. The blood from the huge gun shot wound in his chest had stopped flowing a long time ago. It had soaked into the man's shirt and coat and into the leaves below his body.

"It looks like he has been dead for several hours. Time of death would be in the early hours of this morning," said Andrew before adding, "but we won't know for certain until the post mortem."

shotgun blast	Schuss aus einer Flinte
to soak	*hier:* durchsickern
post mortem	Autopsie
to survey	begutachten
gun club	Schützenverein
⚡ inside job	Werk von Insidern
lack of progress	mangelnder Fortschritt

DI Billington stood back from the corpse and surveyed the scene. Sergeant Fox came to stand by his side. He took one look at the body and said, "I know him, sir."
"You do?"
"Yes, sir. It's George Morris, a local landowner and gun club owner. I met him a few weeks ago. He had come to the station to talk to Detective Singh, the officer in charge of his case. A number of rare, expensive guns had been stolen from his club, sir. Detective Singh thought it may have been an 'inside job'. Mr Morris had come to complain about the lack of progress."
The DI looked thoughtfully at the body. "George Morris. Hmm, I've heard of him."
"I wonder what he was doing in the woods in the middle of the night, sir?" said Danny. "It's such an isolated spot."

"I don't know, Sergeant, but look around you. The **undergrowth** has been disturbed in a wide area around the body. There was a struggle."
"Whatever George Morris found in this clearing last night, I don't think he was expecting it."

Exercise 2: Unscramble. Bringen Sie die Buchstaben in die richtige Reihenfolge!

1. It's such an [teioslad] _isolated_ spot.

2. There was a [ggrutsel] _struggle_ .

3. George had come to [inoacpml] _complain_ about the lack of progress.

4. The [grurwnotedh] _undergrowth_ has been disturbed.

The group of policemen and women huddled together near the entrance to the woods. It was a cold morning and the officers were stamping their feet to keep warm. The police vans that were parked at the side of the road provided a bit of **shelter** from the wind. Detective Inspector Billington had taken care to move his officers far enough away from any members of the public so that he could talk without being **overheard**.

undergrowth	Unterholz
shelter	Schutz, Unterschlupf
to overhear	zufällig hören
victim	Opfer

"Okay, let's start at the beginning. Who found the **victim**?"
A young, tired-looking officer stepped out of the crowd.

"Constable Marsh, sir," he said introducing himself. "I found the body."

DI Billington nodded for him to continue.

"The control centre received a phone call at ten past three this morning. The caller said that a man had been shot in these woods. The control centre sent Constable Roberts and me to investigate." Constable Roberts, an overweight officer with dark circles under his eyes, nodded in agreement.

DI ist die Abkürzung für **Detective Inspector** und entspricht ungefähr dem deutschen Begriff Hauptkommissar.

"Was the caller here when you arrived?"

"No, sir," continued Marsh. "The call was anonymous. The caller wouldn't give his name. He hung up when he was asked again. It was still dark when we arrived, so it took us a while to find the body. We called for an ambulance and we have been here ever since."

Constable Marsh thought about their unpleasant experience in the middle of the night. The woods had been very cold and dark when they arrived. The two policemen had explored the woods with only torches to help them. They had begun to think the call was a fake when they finally found George Morris' body. Constable Marsh had nearly fallen over him in the dark.

"Well done, son," said the DI. "Go home now and get some sleep."

The two Constables headed gratefully back to their car. DI Billington addressed the rest of his officers.

"Sergeant Nicholls, I want you to get onto the control centre. They record

overweight	übergewichtig
to explore	*hier:* durchsuchen
torch	Taschenlampe
grateful	dankbar
clue	Hinweis

every call that comes in. I want a copy of that recording. It's our first clue. Someone was here when George Morris was shot or found him not long afterwards. Who was that person and why didn't they stay around?"

A number of the officers **shrugged**. People who wouldn't give their names to the emergency services usually had something to hide. It wouldn't be an easy job to find their mystery caller.

to shrug	die Schultern zucken
donation	Spende
⚡ to be all over sth.	*hier:* sich über etw. hermachen
to remind sb.	jmd. erinnern

"Sergeant Fox will divide you into groups. I want officers to visit every house nearby to see if anyone saw or heard anything and I want officers searching the rest of the woods for clues. We already have people on their way to tell George Morris' family the news. Sergeant Fox and I will head to the victim's gun club. George Morris was shot. That will be a good place to start."

Exercise 3: Possessive apostrophes. Fügen Sie die Apostrophe an den richtigen Stellen ein.

1. Stephen's boots.

2. The caller's name.

3. Stephen's mother's voice.

4. The two constables' torches.

5. George Morris' family.

Detective Inspector Billington had one last thought for his officers. "George Morris was a well-respected member of Bristol's community. He made generous **donations** to the local school and to other groups in Bristol. People know who he is. The press is going to **be all over** this one. I don't need to **remind you** not to speak to anyone who is not directly involved in the **investigation**. We need to do this correctly and catch this killer quickly."

As Detective Inspector Billington and Sergeant Fox walked back to their car, Danny felt as if they were being watched. **Curious** to see if he was right, he paused and **pretended** to retie his shoe laces while he **scanned** the trees. There was no one to be seen. Seconds later, as he shut the car door, he thought he heard a dog bark.

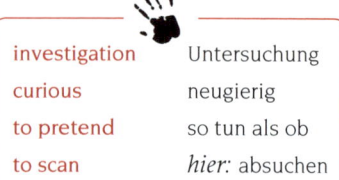

investigation	Untersuchung
curious	neugierig
to pretend	so tun als ob
to scan	*hier:* absuchen

2. A Suspect!

The officers who visited George Morris' family had found it an **upsetting** experience. They hadn't learnt anything new that would help their investigation. George seemed to have been a well-loved man who helped out his community.

As they parked outside the gun club, Detective Billington and Sergeant Fox knew that they needed to find some clues.

"A gun was involved in the murder and guns have recently been stolen from the club. We can't rule out a connection to the gun club," said the DI.

Danny nodded in agreement and led his boss into the club's reception area. Florence, the elderly

upsetting	verstörend
flustered	aufgeregt
to burst into tears	in Tränen ausbrechen
gamekeeper	Wildhüter
groundsman	Platzwart

secretary, was very **flustered** to see the police waiting at her desk. The news of George's death hadn't reached the club yet, and when Detective Billington explained the reason for their visit Florence **burst into tears**.

"I'm sorry to have to tell you this news but we need to ask you some questions about Mr Morris and about the recent break-in at the club."

Once Florence had calmed down slightly she suggested that they speak to Thomas Cruickshank, the club's **gamekeeper** and **groundsman**.

"He will be able to help you more than I can. Thomas has worked here for years and has been friends with George for even longer. I can't imagine what this will do to him."

The thought of Thomas' reaction to the news was enough to start Florence crying again, and it was a few minutes before the policemen could leave her in order to find the gamekeeper.

Exercise 4: Right or wrong? Welche Aussagen sind korrekt? Markieren Sie mit richtig ✓ oder falsch – !

1. Thomas told Florence that George had died. ☐

2. Guns had recently been stolen from the club. ☐

3. No one liked George Morris. ☐

4. Thomas had worked at the gun club for years. ☐

"Thomas Cruickshank?"

The man in the shabby brown overcoat was kneeling by a flowerbed pulling up **weeds**. He adjusted his cap and looked up when he heard his name. His dirty brown dog had been sleeping at his side but stood up growling as the policemen approached.

"I'm Detective Inspector Billington and this is Sergeant Fox. We'd like to ask you some questions about George Morris. I assume you have heard the news?" asked Inspector Billington.

"**Aye**," said Thomas sadly. "His son rang me shortly after the police had left their house. How can I help you?"

Thomas was able to tell the policemen about the layout of the gun club,

| weeds *pl* | Unkraut |
| Aye | Ja |

George's usual routines and **acquaintances**. They were left with a much better idea of the dead man.

"What can you tell us about the recent **robbery**?" asked Sergeant Fox. "Did you see anything or anyone **suspicious** in the area in the days before the guns were stolen?"

"Not really. I spoke to the police at the time. I told them that I had seen some youths hanging around a couple of evenings before the break-in. They were drinking beer and kicking a football around but nothing more **sinister**. I didn't see them that night."

Sergeant Fox continued to ask questions about the break-in as Detective Billington reached into his pocket to answer his ringing phone. Constable Walker, the female officer on the other end of the line, sounded slightly **breathless** with excitement.

"Sir, we've found something."

acquaintance	Bekanntschaft
robbery	Raub
suspicious	verdächtig
sinister	*hier:* schlimm
breathless	atemlos
to shatter	*hier:* (zer)stören
bordering	angrenzend

Danny steered the car through the winding lanes near the gun club. Both men were silent with their own thoughts. The peace was **shattered** by the shrill ring of the DI's mobile phone.

"Detective Inspector Billington speaking."

Danny waited patiently while his boss finished his call.

"That was Sergeant Nicholls calling from the control centre. He has a copy of the anonymous call to the emergency services last night. Our mystery caller sounded like a teenager or young man although Nicholls couldn't be sure. He did say the caller sounded extremely frightened."

Detective Billington and Sergeant Fox found Constable Walker standing on the doorstep of a small cottage **bordering** the woods where the body of George Morris was found.

Exercise 5: Verb forms. Lesen Sie weiter und unterstreichen Sie die richtige Variante!

She **1.** listened / was listening to a **bent** old lady who was talking **animatedly**. Her glasses were perched on the end of her nose. The old lady **2.** was holding / held Constable Walker's arm with one hand and a walking stick in the other. The constable **3.** looked / was looking as if she **4.** was feeling / felt a bit trapped. The look of **relief** on her face **5.** was / has been obvious when she saw the two policemen walk up the garden path to join her. After she **6.** was introducing / had introduced them, Constable Walker turned to the elderly lady.

"Mrs…"
"Just call me Peggy."
"Peggy, could you please tell the Detective what you have just told me."
"Well, young man, as I was just telling the constable here, I suffer badly from arthritis. Terrible it is! It keeps me awake a lot of the time. I hope you never suffer from it young man. The things I could tell you…"
Constable Walker rolled her eyes at the good-looking Sergeant Fox. He **winked** at her and she **blushed**. He could imagine how

bent	gebeugt
animatedly	angeregt
relief	Erleichterung
to wink	zuzwinkern
to blush	erröten

hard it had been to listen politely to the old lady's **ramblings**.

"Yes, as I was saying, last night I was getting a drink of water so I could take my **painkillers**. You can see the woods from my kitchen window. It must have been, oh, about three o'clock this morning. I remember because my cat was awake too and she always wakes up around three..."

ramblings *pl*	Gefasel, Geschwafel
painkiller	Schmerzmittel
shifty	durchtrieben
↯ to be up to no good	nichts Gutes vorhaben
to trespass	widerrechtlich betreten
pheasant	Fasan

"Peggy," reminded Constable Walker, "please tell Detective Billington what you heard."

"A gun shot!" she paused for dramatic effect. "Then I saw that boy running from the woods."

"Which boy?" asked the DI.

"Stephen McDougal. A **shifty** boy from the next street. He hangs around on his own a lot. He has no friends. He's obviously **up to no good!**"

Danny Fox was taking notes.

> In Großbritannien spielt die Jagd nach wie vor eine große Rolle. Besonders Fasane sind ein beliebtes Beutetier.

"And," continued Peggy, "I know that George Morris recently had words with Stephen's parents about his **trespassing** in the woods. Thomas the gamekeeper had seen him there several times and thought the boy might be stealing **pheasants**[i]."

"What?" Peggy peered up at Constable Walker. "Speak up, dear."

Constable Walker spoke very loudly and slowly. "Tell Detective Billington what you heard."

"When, dear?"

Constable Walker rolled her eyes in frustration.

"Last night, Peggy. What did you hear?"

Exercise 6: Fill in the blanks. Finden Sie das passende Verb und setzen Sie es in die korrekte Zeitform!

call   exchange   do not   look   be

After Constable Walker had taken Peggy back into her house to sit down, Detective Billington and Sergeant Fox 1. _exchanged_ looks. The old woman really had been rambling. It was also quite obvious that she was a bit deaf and that her eyesight wasn't brilliant. How good a **witness** 2. _was_ she? Just then they were 3. _called_ by a young woman in the front garden of the house next door.

"Er, excuse me officers. I 4. _didn't_ mean to overhear but could I have a word?"

The policemen walked round the hedge separating them to join the woman in her garden. She was young, blonde and 5. _looked_ tired.

"Hi, I'm Gemma. I was awake at around three, too. I have a new baby and she doesn't let me get a lot of sleep! I heard the gun shot and when I looked out of my window, I saw a man running from the woods. It was too dark for me to see who it was, though."
"This must be the same person Peggy saw!" exclaimed Sergeant Fox.
"Possibly," said Gemma slowly. "I heard you talking to Peggy. I

should warn you, she's a lovely lady but once she gets an idea in her head then you can't **change her mind**.

DI Billington smiled **sympathetically**.

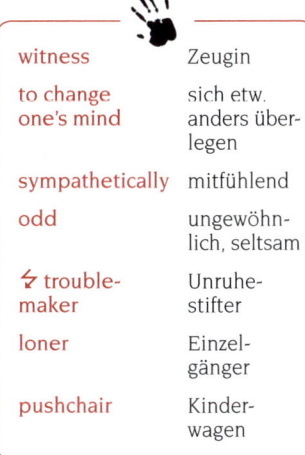

witness	Zeugin
to change one's mind	sich etw. anders überlegen
sympathetically	mitfühlend
odd	ungewöhnlich, seltsam
⚡ troublemaker	Unruhestifter
loner	Einzelgänger
pushchair	Kinderwagen

"She has told me that she has seen Stephen McDougal going in and out of the woods at **odd** times," continued Gemma. "She may have got this confused with last night. Also, recently she has decided that Stephen is a **troublemaker**. If you believe everything she says, then he is some sort of criminal mastermind or terrorist!"

"What do you think?" asked DI Billington.

"He seems harmless to me. A bit of a **loner** but he has never done anything to make me worry. He helped me with my baby's **pushchair** once and he was very polite."

Just then the sound of a baby's cry came from the house. Gemma sighed.

"Sorry, I have to go."

The policemen thanked her for her help and as they returned to their car, Detective Inspector Billington turned to his sergeant.

"Danny, we need to speak to this Stephen McDougal. He's currently our only suspect. Suspicious behaviour, history of trespassing, one witness and we know it was a young man who made the call to the emergency services. Let's go."

3. Unexpected Visitors

Stephen McDougal lived in a small cottage with his parents. There was nothing interesting or **remarkable** about it. There was nothing to say this might be the home of their murderer. A short, red-faced man opened the door to them.

"What has the stupid boy done now?" he said angrily when he saw the policemen.

Sergeant Fox was a bit shocked at the man's reaction.

"Er, nothing that we know of, sir. We would just like to talk to Stephen McDougal. We understand he lives here. Is he your son?"

remarkable	auffallend, bemerkenswert
to snort	schnauben
mousy	farblos
to stammer	stottern
timidly	schüchtern
unsettled	unruhig
to accuse	beschuldigen
stern	ernst

The man **snorted**.

"No, thankfully. My name is Arthur Evans. Stephen is my stepson. My wife June is his mother."

Arthur gestured to a small **mousy** woman the officers could see looking nervously over the man's shoulder.

"Please come in," she **stammered**. "Stephen is in the back room."

DI Billington and Sergeant Fox followed June down the hall. At the living room door she turned and looked **timidly** at Detective Billington.

"Please don't upset him, Officers. He's a good boy and was very **unsettled** after George Morris came to the house and **accused** him of trespassing. Did you know?"

"No Ma'am, we hadn't realized that Mr Morris came here. How long ago did this happen?"

"Well, it was a few weeks ago now. George was very nice about it, really, but quite stern. Stephen was quiet and distant for days afterwards. He wouldn't talk to us about it."

George's mother didn't seem to realize that she wasn't helping her son's situation. Stephen got to his feet when the officers entered the room. He was a slim boy of about sixteen, wearing jeans and a dark T-shirt. His brown hair was a little too long and fell forwards over his face.

Exercise 7: Multiple choice. Welcher Satz ist korrekt? Kreuzen Sie an!

1. a) ☒ "What has the stupid boy done now?"
   b) ☐ "What did the stupid boy do now?"

2. a) ☐ Nothing that we now of, sir.
   b) ☒ Nothing that we know of, sir.

3. a) ☐ Stephen has been quiet and distant for days afterwards.
   b) ☒ Stephen was quiet and distant for days afterwards.

4. a) ☒ He got to his feet when the officers entered the room.
   b) ☐ He got too his feet when the officers entered the room.

"What's going on, Mum?"

"It's nothing to worry about love," June said gently. "The officers just want to ask you some questions about George Morris. You know they found his body in the woods this morning."

>
> **Information** wird im Englischen grundsätzlich nur im Singular verwendet. Im Deutschen hingegen können wir den Begriff auch im Plural verwenden.

Stephen's face went white at the mention of George Morris.

"We also want to talk to you about some guns that have been stolen from the club."

"What?" said Stephen shocked. "I don't know anything about stolen guns!"

"Of course you don't," snorted Arthur.

Detective Inspector Billington glared at him.

"Stephen, we just want some information. No one is accusing you of anything at the moment."

"I haven't done anything!" cried Stephen in frustration.

gently	sanft, zärtlich
at the mention	bei der Erwähnung
to glare at sb./sth.	etw./jmd. wütend anstarren
agitated	aufgeregt

"Calm down, son," said Danny. "We've got a witness who said that she saw you running out of the woods on the night of George's murder."

"I wasn't there! It wasn't me. They must have made a mistake!"

"Okay, then tell us exactly where you were at around 3 a.m. this morning." Stephen's mum spoke up.

"He was in bed. Weren't you, Stephen?"

"Yes, of course," Stephen replied. But he wouldn't meet the policemen's eyes.

"What are you hiding, son?" asked Detective Billington gently.

"Nothing!" shouted Stephen, suddenly very agitated. "I wasn't there. I don't know anything about George Morris!"

Sergeant Fox stepped towards Stephen to try to calm him down. As he put his hand on the young man's shoulder, Stephen suddenly gave him a big push.

"No!"

Stephen spun around and fled out of the back door of the cottage. It took Danny Fox a second to get his balance and then he ran after him. He caught a glimpse of Stephen's T-shirt as he disappeared into the woods at the back of the property.

Exercise 8: Odd one out. Welches Wort ist das „schwarze Schaf"? Unterstreichen Sie!

1. mention | say | ~~hear~~ | speak

2. suspicious | sinister | shifty | ~~sympathetic~~

3. detective | ~~witness~~ | sergeant | inspector

4. frustrated | agitated | ~~calm~~ | animated

"He's a good lad officers, honestly! He wouldn't hurt anyone," protested June.

"Running away from the police never looks good," replied Detective Billington.

to catch a glimpse	einen Blick erhaschen
property	Grundstück
lad	Junge
to mutter	grummeln
to hiss	zischen

"How are we supposed to know what the boy is doing when he is out of the cottage?" muttered Stephen's stepdad.

"Shut up, Arthur," hissed June.

Arthur looked at her shocked. He obviously wasn't used to her answering back.

Minutes later Danny arrived back in the cottage alone and shook his head at his superior.

"I've lost him."

Stephen ran as fast as he could. Once he was certain he had lost his pursuer, he crept silently back towards the cottage. He lay on his stomach in the bushes at the edge of the woods. He needed to know what was happening and he knew the policemen had to leave eventually.

Stephen's patience was rewarded when the cottage door opened. He could see the two officers talking to his mother on the doorstep. Their voices floated back to him.

"Your son is hiding something, Mrs Evans. Please call us as soon as he reappears. Don't make us come looking for him."

He couldn't hear his mother's reply as she shut the door firmly behind them.

As the policemen got into their car, DI Billington gave his orders.

superior	Vorgesetzter
pursuer	Verfolger
to creep	schleichen, kriechen
patience	Geduld
to reward	belohnen
patrol car	Streifenwagen
to occur to sb.	jmd. einfallen
to hold a grudge	einen Groll hegen
bully	Tyrann

"Call the station, Danny. I want Stephen McDougal's description given to every patrol car in the area. If anyone sees him, they should stop him immediately. I want to talk to that young man. Right, it's been a long day. Let's finish for tonight."

Very early the next morning, the DI and sergeant went back to the murder scene. The detective liked to visit the scene of crime again to see if anything new would occur to him. The sun hadn't yet risen fully and the clearing was still quite dark and full of shadows.

"What are we missing, Danny?" he asked softly.

Exercise 9: Fill in the blanks. Ergänzen Sie die Aussagen und enträtseln Sie das Lösungswort!

1. Stephen hid in the w o o d s
2. Stephen moved s i l e n t l y, without making a noise.
3. Stephen and his parents lived in a c o t t a g e
4. Stephen is Arthur's s t e p s o n
5. Sergeant Fox is a p o l i c e man
6. DI Billington is Danny's s u p e r i o r
7. Sergeant Fox s h o o k his head.

Lösung: w i t n e s s

"I don't know, sir. Everyone who knew George Morris seems to have liked him. We haven't been able to find any enemies who might hold a grudge. And then there is Stephen. He is definitely hiding something but he seems scared to me. You saw his room, sir, all those nature books. He is a loner who prefers nature to people."
"You're right. And with a bully like Arthur Evans for a stepdad, I'm not surprised," DI Billington commented.
"Exactly. I just can't see Stephen as the murderer. And why would George Morris be meeting a sixteen-year-old boy in the woods in the middle of the night?"

Exercise 10: Prepositions. Ergänzen Sie den Text mit den richtigen Präpositionen!

| at | from | in | of | in | out |

Before the DI could answer, the two men became aware of an odd snuffling sound and a **rustling** **1.** _in_ the undergrowth. They both fell silent and stood very still. To their amazement some leaves were pushed aside and a **badger** appeared **2.** _from_ under a bush. Its black and white face stood **3.** _out_ in the half-light **4.** _of_ the early morning. For a long moment the badger and the policemen looked **5.** _at_ each other **6.** _in_ surprise.

Then the quiet of the woods was disturbed by the loud ringing of Sergeant Fox's mobile phone. He **frantically** searched through his pockets. He was hoping to turn it off before it scared off the badger, but he was too late, and they saw the badger's grey **fur** disappearing quickly back into the undergrowth.

rustling	Rascheln
badger	Dachs
frantically	verzweifelt
fur	Fell

Danny Fox put the phone to his ear in disappointment. He listened carefully before turning to his boss with growing excitement.
"Guess who is a member of George Morris' gun club!"

 A Twist

"This makes the decision for us, Danny," said DI Billington. "We need to find Stephen. The boy might be frightened, but he could also be a murderer. Let's go."

Stephen answered the cottage door to Sergeant Fox's knock. His face lost all colour when he realized who it was. He looked back into the cottage as if he was thinking of running again. Sergeant Fox immediately grabbed hold of his arm.

"Don't even think about it. You won't be getting away this time."

"Put the **handcuffs** on him, Danny," said the Detective Inspector.

The boy was **literally** shaking with fear.

handcuffs *pl*	Handschellen
literally	buchstäblich
tea towel	Geschirrtuch
half-shaved	halb rasiert
shaving foam	Rasierschaum

As the cold metal fastened around his wrists, Stephen panicked.

"Mum! Mum! Don't let them take me."

June Evans came running, a damp **tea towel** still in her hands. She stared in horror at the policemen with their hands on her child.

"What's going on? What are you doing to my son?"

Arthur Evans appeared at the top of the stairs. His face was **half-shaved** and he still had **shaving foam** on his left ear.

"You again!" he shouted. "Why are you back?"

Detective Inspector Billington nodded his head in a greeting.

"Mr Evans, we know you are a member of George Morris' gun club and keep a gun at home. Stephen was seen running away from the

scene of the murder. He has access to a gun. He has some very serious questions to answer."
Arthur snorted as he came down the stairs to join them.
"The boy is stupid but he's not violent. He wouldn't have the courage. Don't make me laugh."
Arthur came to stand next to his wife and tried to look **threatening**.
"We know you own a gun, Mr Evans. We would like to see it," said DI Billington calmly. "Does Stephen have access to your gun? Could he have taken it without your knowledge?"
Arthur looked **indignant**.
"The little **fool** has never touched my gun. He wouldn't dare! I know the rules. My gun is properly locked away and the only key is always in my pocket. There is no way he can get to it. I'm the only one who uses it."
"We still need to see it, Mr Evans."

Exercise 11: Opposites. Finden Sie das Gegenteil der Begriffe!

1. peaceful — *threatening*
2. clever — *dumb*
3. sunset — *sunrise*
4. calm — *loud / indignant*
5. fear — *courage*
6. patience — *impatience*

Arthur Evans led the way to the back of the cottage and to a tall wooden cabinet in the corner of the lounge. He reluctantly handed Sergeant Fox the key. Danny unlocked the door and carefully lifted the gun out of its cabinet.

threatening	bedrohlich
indignant	empört
fool	Narr, Trottel

"It's a shotgun, sir, and it looks like there is gunpowder residue on the gun barrel. This could mean it has recently been fired."

"Hmm, this changes things," said DI Billington. "Where were you, Mr Evans around 3 a.m. on the night George Morris was murdered?"

"I was in bed. Where do you think I would be at that time of night?"

"Is there anyone that can confirm this?"

Arthur nodded confidently at his wife.

"June can tell you. I never left the bedroom all night."

Detective Inspector Billington turned to the small anxious woman standing next to her son.

"Is this true, Mrs Evans?"

She hesitated and looked at her red-faced bully of a husband. Then slowly she shook her head.

"He was out," she whispered. "He took his shotgun. He told me he was shooting rabbits, but I don't know where he went."

Arthur let out a tremendous shout and leapt towards his wife.

"Why you...."

DI Billington stepped between them. June hid behind him.

"I suggest you calm down, sir."

"Calm down! Calm down?"

Arthur's voice was loud and indignant.

cabinet	Schrank
reluctantly	widerwillig
residue	Rest
barrel	Gewehrlauf
to confirm	bestätigen
confidently	selbstsicher
anxious	ängstlich
tremendous	enorm, gewaltig

"I can't believe that you think I killed the man. George Morris was a **liar** and a **cheat**. He deserved everything he got. He never paid me for the building work I did for him last summer. He **threatened** to take me to court. I did everything he had asked for. It's not my fault the gun club committee didn't like it. I had **kept my side of the bargain**. Is it too much to expect to get paid for the work I have done?"

"Did you ever approach George and ask to be paid?"

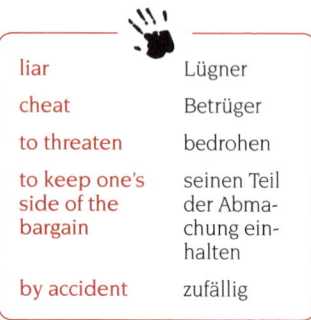

liar	Lügner
cheat	Betrüger
to threaten	bedrohen
to keep one's side of the bargain	seinen Teil der Abmachung einhalten
by accident	zufällig

Exercise 12: Verb forms. Lesen Sie weiter und setzen Sie die korrekte Verbform ein!

"Too right I did. He **1. stop** _stopped_ answering my phone calls so I **2. go** _went_ _____ to see him at his house. His wife wouldn't let me in, but I **3. shout** _shouted_ and shouted until he **4. come** _came_ to the door. I **5. demand** _demanded_ my money and he threatened to set his dogs on me. His dogs! I should have called the police."

DI Billington gave the man a long, intense look.

"It seems you had a good reason to be angry with him. So what happened on the night George died? Did you meet **by accident** when you were out hunting rabbits? Did you have an argument and you lost your temper?"

Arthur began to see where the conversation was heading. He tried to change his voice from a shout and to control his temper.

"Now wait a minute. I didn't like the man and he owed me a lot of money, but I didn't kill him."

"You went to his house, Mr Evans. You were aggressive and you obviously have a fierce temper. Did you lose control and kill him when he wouldn't give you what you wanted?"

Arthur's face went purple.

"Now listen here, you idiot," he shouted. "I did not kill that cheat. How dare you come to my home and accuse me of murder! Get out of my house before I throw you out!"

"No, sir. We will be leaving, but I think you will be coming with us."

Detective Inspector Billington stared solemnly at the man in front of him. Arthur Evans suddenly didn't look like such an aggressive bully. For once there was a hint of fear in his eyes. He looked to his wife for support, but she was staring at her feet and weeping quietly. She wouldn't raise her head.

to lose one's temper	die Beherrschung verlieren
fierce	wild, heftig
solemnly	ernst
hint	Hauch
support	Unterstützung
evidence	Beweis
sobbing	schluchzend

"June?"

Arthur was unusually quiet as the Detective Inspector slipped the handcuffs around his wrists.

"Arthur Evans, I am arresting you for the murder of George Morris. You do not have to say anything, but anything you do say can be used as evidence against you."

Sergeant Fox released Stephen. The young man stood with his arm around his sobbing mother's shoulders as the policemen led his stepfather outside to the waiting police car.

Exercise 13: Questions to the text. Beantworten Sie die Fragen!

1. Who did the policemen arrest first?

   They arrested Stephen first.

2. Where did Arthur tell his wife he was going on the night of the murder?

   Arthur told his wife he was going to hunt rabbits

3. Why didn't Arthur like George?

   He didn't get his money from him.

4. Why was Arthur angry with his wife?

   She told the policemen the truth.

 # Guilty

DI Billington and Sergeant Fox were working on their **paperwork** back at the police station when Danny let out a sigh of disappointment.

"I have the lab report on Arthur Evans' shotgun here, sir. It says the gun has been recently fired, but it is not our murder weapon. It seems he was telling the truth about hunting rabbits."

"It looks that way, Danny," agreed the DI, "We don't have any more evidence against him. We will have to release him."

"So where does this leave us, sir? We're right back at the beginning."

"Not necessarily. I think Stephen may still have some answers for us. Maybe we've just been asking the wrong questions."

Danny looked at his boss in **confusion**.

"What do you mean?"

"The boy has been in the woods and he is hiding something. We just need to work out what and why he won't tell us."

They were **interrupted** by a call from the station's receptionist. "Stephen McDougal and his mother are here and asking to speak to you."

Stephen and his mother were waiting at the reception desk. Away from her husband, Mrs Evans seemed to have grown more confident.

"Officers, Stephen has something to tell you."

The boy looked terrified.

"Okay," said DI Billington. "We need to do this formally. Follow me, please."

paperwork	Papierkram
confusion	Verwirrung
to interrupt	unterbrechen

With Danny close behind him, the policeman led Stephen and his mother through the station and into an interview room. Once they were sitting down, Sergeant Fox turned on the tape recorder.

"This is an interview with Stephen McDougal. The police officers present are Detective Inspector Charles Billington and Sergeant Daniel Fox. Stephen's mother June Evans is also here."

"Now," said the DI, "what is it you have come to say?"

Stephen's pale face went even whiter. He shrank into his seat. June took his hand and gave it an encouraging squeeze.

"It's alright, sweetheart. Nothing is going to happen to you. Now you must tell the officers what happened."

Stephen cleared his throat and began to speak in a quiet, trembling voice. He fiddled nervously with his fingers as he spoke.

"I was in the woods the night George Morris was killed."

Exercise 14: Adjectives. Ergänzen Sie die fehlenden Formen!

1. pale	paler	palest
2. close	closer	closest
3. gentle	gentler	gentlest
4. bad	worse	worst
5. quiet	quieter	quietest
6. formal	more formal	most formal
7. confident	more confident	most confident

The policemen exchanged a glance. Maybe this was the break they had been looking for. Stephen noticed the look.

"But I wasn't doing anything wrong!" he said earnestly. "Well, I know I wasn't supposed to be there. George had already warned me to stay away, but I wasn't hurting anyone."

"Let's not worry about that now," said Detective Inspector Billington in a sympathetic voice. "What were you doing in the woods, Stephen?"

interview room	Verhörraum
tape recorder	Kassettenrekorder
to shrink	*hier:* kleiner werden
to fiddle	*hier:* herumspielen

The boy gave his mum a guilty look.

"I've been **sneaking out** at night," he admitted. "My mum and Arthur didn't know. A few weeks ago, I was out for a walk one day and I found a big hole dug into an **earth bank**. I thought something might live there, so I went back that night. It was a **badger's sett** and I watched them as they came out to hunt. I've been going back several nights a week since then."

"And that is why you were there the night George Morris was killed?"

"Yes. I know he told me to keep out of the woods. But I thought if I went at night then it would be okay. No one would ever know."

"Is this why you wouldn't speak to us before? You thought you would be in trouble?"

Again Stephen nodded **miserably**.

"Yes, and I was scared."

"Why scared? Did you see something the night George died? Did you see who murdered him?"

to sneak out	sich herausschleichen
earth bank	Erdhügel
badger's sett	Dachsbau
miserably	unglücklich
comfortingly	tröstend

Stephen looked as if he wanted to run away or to disappear.

"Go on, love," smiled June **comfortingly**. "You need to tell them what you know."

Exercise 15: Adverbs. Unterstreichen Sie alle Adverbien!

1. "Go on, Stephen," his mother prompted <u>gently.</u> "Tell the officers what you told me."

2. He fiddled <u>nervously</u> with his fingers as he spoke.

3. "But I wasn't doing anything wrong!" he said <u>earnestly.</u>

4. Again Stephen nodded <u>miserably.</u>

5. "Go on, love," smiled June <u>comfortingly.</u> "You need to tell them what you know."

The boy **pulled himself together** and continued.
"I was hiding in the bushes on the edge of the clearing. I didn't hear the men until it was too late for me to get away ⓘ. I couldn't move without them hearing or seeing me."
"What happened next?" asked Sergeant Fox.
"Their voices were quiet, but I could hear them coming closer. It was so dark I couldn't see them at first. Then they stepped out into the clearing and the moon shone on them."
"How many men were there and what did they look like?"
"There were two men to start with. They were wearing dark clothing and their hats were pulled down low. I couldn't see their faces. They just stood there like they were waiting for something."
The policemen nodded for him to keep talking.

> Weitere Wendungen mit dem Verb **get** sind:
> to get back — zurückkommen
> to get around — herumkommen

"Then a third man appeared. He was carrying a big heavy bag. The first two men went to meet him. I couldn't hear what they were saying. The third man opened the bag to show them the contents. I couldn't see at first but then the moon shone on it and I could see as he took out a large, antique-looking gun."

⚡ to pull one-self together	sich zusammenreißen
content	Inhalt
wad	Bündel
to betray	betrügen

"The stolen guns!" breathed Sergeant Fox.

"The men were exchanging a big wad of money when George Morris arrived. He must have seen the men's cars on the edge of the woods. He had come to see who was on his land. He was so angry when he recognized the man selling the guns. There was a big argument. George was furious. He kept shouting 'How could you betray me like this, after all this time?' He wanted them to give him the guns but they wouldn't. I suppose George was used to people doing as he told them. When they refused, he tried to take the guns. There was a fight. The third man still had the gun in his hand. As George grabbed him, the gun went off."

Exercise 16: Match up the words. Ordnen Sie den Wörtern die passende Definition zu!

1. [c] antique   a) to say no

2. [d] badger   b) very angry

3. [a] refuse   c) a valuable, old object

4. [b] furious   d) an animal with a black and white face

Stephen shut his eyes at the horrible memory.

"George fell to the floor. There was so much blood," he whispered. "The three men ran away into the woods."

"You're doing well, son," smiled DI Billington. "What happened next?"

Exercise 17: Choose the correct alternative. Lesen Sie weiter und unterstreichen Sie die richtige Variante!

"I waited until I was sure they had gone. Then I 1. went / had gone to see George. I 2. doesn't / didn't know what to do. I knew he was dead but I couldn't just 3. let / leave him there. I used my mobile phone to call for help. I waited 4. at / in the bushes until the police officers found him. Then I ran home."

"Why didn't you wait and talk to the police, Stephen?"

"I was scared. I wasn't supposed to be 5. here / there and I was worried they 6. could / would think I had done it."

"7. Have / Did you recognize any of the men, Stephen?" DI Billington asked. The boy nodded weakly.

"Yes, just one, the man 8. who / which shot George."

Thomas Cruickshank pulled his cap tightly down on the top of his head and stepped out into the gardens. He turned and locked the door of the shed at the back of the gun club. His shotgun was held loosely over his arm. As he moved out of the shadows of the doorway, his dog growled. Then he heard it.

to surround — umzingeln

"Drop your weapon, Mr Cruickshank, and put your hands on your head. We have you **surrounded**!"

The Spy's Last Shot

Gina Billy

1 Shots in the Dark

Brian Buckley was filling another glass with local beer in his pub on Tomb Street. It had been busy for a Tuesday night in Belfast, but business was finally slowing down. Brian finished pulling the pint for one of his last customers and ran a hand through his short grey hair. He looked up at the clock on the wall. There was still half an hour until closing time. But even then, his work day wouldn't be finished. He thought about the secret meeting that was planned for later that night. Hopefully, both of the ladies he was expecting would arrive at the pub on time and everything would go as planned. But now he needed to serve the round of drinks to the group of men sitting at the other end of the bar. The five of them were all regulars at "Buckley's". They came to the pub several nights a week to drink and talk about things like local events, world news or sport. Tonight, they were going on about a group of scientists and researchers visiting Belfast from its twin city Hefei in China. Brian was secretly very interested in their conversation, and he was listening carefully as he brought over their drinks.

"Well, if you ask me, the Lord Mayor's just wasting our money giving a big party tonight for those foreigners," said Thomas McNeil. Brian put the pints down in front of them and Thomas continued giving his opinion.

to pull a pint	ein Bier zapfen
regulars *pl*	Stammgäste
⚡ to go on about sth.	sich über etw. auslassen
twin city	Partnerstadt
Lord Mayor	Oberbürgermeister

"And besides, everybody knows they're just coming over here to steal our business secrets." Thomas raised his glass and said "cheers".

Then Jerry Ryan, a younger man, spoke up.

"Well, I don't know about that, Thomas. I think it's a **grand** thing for Belfast to have visitors. After all, we had enough years during **the Troubles** when nobody felt safe coming here."

When Ryan said "The Troubles", the men suddenly became quiet.

grand *IRL*	großartig
the Troubles *pl*	der Nordirlandkonflikt
industrial espionage	Wirtschaftsspionage

They didn't like thinking about the time of terror in the past. Thomas quickly turned the conversation back to China.

"Remember what Arthur Stevens told us a few weeks ago? He said his engineering company was losing millions of pounds every year because of ... what was it? Oh yes, '**industrial espionage**'.

Exercise 1: Prepositions. Lesen Sie weiter und ergänzen Sie die fehlenden Präpositionen!

~~on~~   ~~into~~   ~~about~~   ~~of~~   ~~with~~   ~~in~~

Brian really didn't want to talk **1.** *about* that topic **2.** *with* his regulars. Before he could think **3.** *of* a way to change the subject, the bell hanging **4.** *on* the pub's front door rang. A man dressed **5.** *in* a dark business suit walked **6.** *into* the pub.

He looked oriental. The other guests immediately stopped talking about the Chinese and stealing secrets. The man said "good evening." Then he sat down at the other end of the bar and Brian went over to take his order.

The glass of champagne in Zheng Cai's hand was almost empty. She had another look at her watch. It was almost time for her to leave the Lord Mayor's reception. Zheng Cai smiled politely up at her boss Arthur Stevens and the visiting Chinese computer expert, Dr. Liu Jing.

reception	Empfang
politely	höflich
stained-glass	Buntglas
magnificent	prachtvoll, großartig
City Hall	Rathaus
dressed up	aufgetakelt, schick angezogen
to sip	nippen
⚡ to feel a bit under the weather	sich etw. angeschlagen fühlen

The three of them were standing under one of the seven beautiful stained-glass windows in the Great Hall. It was the most magnificent of the three reception rooms at Belfast's City Hall. Tonight it was filled with local politicians, business leaders and the guests from Hefei. They were all dressed up and most of them were sipping champagne out of expensive crystal glasses. The Lord Mayor had just finished giving a long speech. Now, Mr Stevens was telling Dr. Liu about his business interests in China.

Cai was trying very hard to seem interested, but her thoughts were far away. In just half an hour, she was meeting her contact again. It would be the third – and hopefully last – of their very risky meetings. Cai was nervous.

"And you, Ms Zheng? Would you also like some more?"

Dr. Liu was looking at Cai's empty glass.

"Oh, that's very kind of you, Dr. Liu, but actually, I'm feeling a bit under the weather. In fact, I think I really should go home."

"That's a great pity, Ms Zheng. I was looking forward to, um, getting to know you better." Dr. Liu looked quite disappointed.

"I hope you haven't got a **bug**, Cai." Mr Stevens' comment made Cai's heart beat faster. She did have a bug, but not the kind Mr Stevens meant. The bug she had was used for secretly recording people's conversations.

bug	*hier:* Bazillus; Wanze
better to be safe than sorry	Vorsicht ist besser als Nachsicht

"Oh, I'm sure I'll be fine in the morning, sir," she promised. "After all, I wouldn't want to miss showing Dr. Liu and the other guests from Hefei around the company tomorrow." Cai said goodbye to the two men and walked to the main exit.

Exercise 2: Synonyms. Welche Wörter gehören zusammen? Ordnen Sie zu!

1. [b] risky   a) worried
2. [c] magnificent   b) dangerous
3. [d] kind   c) splendid
4. [a] nervous   d) nice

Across the room, a blonde woman wearing a blue, silk dress watched Cai make her departure. The Lord Mayor's special assistant, Tamsin O'Reilly waited until Cai was out of the room. Then she pulled a tiny mobile phone from her evening bag and quickly texted a message. The words on the display read "she's on her way." Tamsin hit the send key and then made sure to delete the message from her phone – **better safe than sorry**, she thought.

"Sorry, sir, what did you say? I couldn't quite hear your order."
At first, the stranger at the bar didn't answer Brian's question. He was busy reading a message that had just arrived on his mobile. After he put the phone back in his pocket, the man apologized and spoke up.
"Pardon me. I'll have a **pint** of Guinness and a shot of your best whiskey, please." The man spoke with a heavy Chinese accent.
Brian quickly prepared and served the drinks.
"Can I get you anything else, sir? It's almost time for **last orders**."
"Well, actually, you can Mr Buckley, or should I call you 'Buckles'? You can call last orders right now. Your operation is about to go out of business. Permanently."
The man said these words very quietly and then pulled back the coat that was covering one of his hands. In it, he was holding a gun. It was pointed directly at Brian.

pint	*hier:* Glas
last orders	letzte Bestellung (vor Schließung des Pubs)
disbelief	Zweifel, Unglaube
Superintendent	Hauptkommissar
investigation	Ermittlung
elderly	ältere(r, s)

"Brian Buckley?" Chief Inspector Daniel Bowles shook his head in **disbelief** at his boss, **Superintendent** Abigail Collins.
The two members of the Police Service of Northern Ireland, also known as PSNI, were standing in a corner of the Great Hall. From here, they could see all the guests at the Lord Mayor's reception.
"You mean you are leaving me here alone because 'Buckles' thinks he's discovered something that could help our **investigation** into industrial espionage?"
Abigail Collins could understand that Bowles was sceptical. He was a new member of the small team of PSNI officers who knew that Brian Buckley was more than an **elderly** pub owner. Brian worked

undercover for the United Kingdom's Security Service. Based in London, the agency was also known as MI5 [i]. Its responsibilities included investigating terrorism, espionage and economic crimes in the United Kingdom.

> [i] MI5 ist die Abkürzung von **Military Intelligence, Section Five**. Die Aufgabe des Inlandsgeheimdienstes ist der Schutz der Demokratie.

"Look, Bowles. I don't have much time left before I need to go and meet Brian. Just remember, for many years he gave us lots of **valuable** information."

"Well, he hasn't been much help lately." Bowles still wasn't convinced. "How many details did he tell you on the phone?"

"He didn't say much, just that he had 'something big' and that I should meet him at the pub around 11:30 tonight. That means I need to be on my way. **Meanwhile**, you keep an eye on things here." Bowles looked around at the large number of people still at the reception. He saw the Lord Mayor's attractive assistant Tamsin O'Reilly talking with one of the Chinese guests.

"Bowles! That wasn't what I meant by 'keeping an eye on things'!"

| valuable | wertvoll |
| meanwhile | währenddessen |

"Certainly not, Superintendent. And I wasn't..."

"Yes, you were, but never mind. Just think about why you're here, will you?"

Brian didn't have time to think about how the mysterious Chinese man knew his code name "Buckles". Right now, he had more important things on his mind. He took a deep breath to calm himself and rang the bell on the bar that signalled last orders.

His regulars weren't pleased to hear the sound. And Brian's next words didn't make them any happier.

"Drink up, lads. I'm closing down a bit earlier tonight."

Brian ignored their protests and watched them down their drinks. Then he followed them to the door and wished them all a good night. Luckily, they were all quite tipsy and didn't notice that the Chinese man wasn't with them.

Brian took the sign on the door and turned it over to the "sorry, we're closed" side. But he remembered to hang it at an angle. He could hear the stranger breathing heavily behind him. Then he heard the gun click. Time was running out and Brian knew he had only one chance. Suddenly, he kicked back with his left foot while whirling around on his right one. His foot landed directly in the man's stomach and Brian tried to get control of the gun. He was too late. The man pulled the trigger and Brian felt the bullet fly past his head. Brian tackled the man and finally got his hand on the gun. Then another shot rang out, and then another.

⚡ to down drinks	Getränke hinunterkippen
tipsy	beschwipst
at an angle	schief
to whirl around	sich schnell drehen
to pull the trigger	den Abzug betätigen, abdrücken
to tackle	angreifen

Exercise 3: Questions. Ergänzen Sie das richtige Fragewort!

1. _____ was wearing a blue, silk dress?

2. _____ were Abigail and Bowles standing?

3. _____ did Brian tell Abigail?

4. _____ did Brian place the sign on the door?

Dead Shot

The Prince Albert Memorial Clock Tower bell rang the half hour just as Cai reached Tomb Street. She had decided not to take a taxi. It was only a 15-minute walk from City Hall at Donegall Square to "Buckley's", and the night air helped steady her nerves and clear her head. Cai was certain now that she was doing the right thing. A light rain started falling just as she was about to cross the street to the

memorial	Gedenkstätte
to steady	beruhigen
to backfire	fehlzünden
downpour	Platzregen

pub. But a loud noise made her stop. It had sounded like a motor backfiring, but there weren't any cars or lorries around. Then Cai heard the sound two more times. Her eyes opened wide in shock. Those were gunshots and they were coming from inside the pub!

Cai was scared to death and didn't know what to do. That's when she panicked and began running back the way she had just come. Her high-heeled shoes slipped on the now wet pavement and she almost fell, but she caught her balance and started running again. The light rain quickly turned into a heavy downpour. Her heels clicked louder and louder. Cai's only thought was to get as far away from the pub as possible. She didn't see a tall man step out of the shadow of the Royal Mail building at the end of the street. The soles of his heavy boots squeaked on the pavement as he began to follow her. But Cai could only hear the sound of the rain, her shoes and her heartbeat as she turned the corner back onto Albert Square.

Exercise 4: Past tense verbs. Lesen Sie weiter und setzen Sie die korrekte Verbform ein!

Abigail's eyes **1. turn** _____ automatically towards the dark-haired woman running around the corner. The poor girl's been caught in the rain without an umbrella, she **2. think** _____. Then she **3. see** _____ a man also walking in the same direction. Abigail **4. be** _____ glad to be nice and dry in her old red mini. She **5. start** _____ looking for a place to park the car. Oh, good. There **6. be** _____ a free spot directly across the street from the pub. That was lucky! Two of Belfast's most popular nightclubs **7. be** _____ in Tomb Street and parking **8. be** _____ often a big problem.

Before getting out of the car, Abigail looked over at "Buckley's". That was strange. There were no lights on inside. Her eyes moved to the front door and that's when she saw the "closed" sign hanging at an angle. Abigail **caught her breath**. The sign's position meant "I'm in trouble and need help." In all their years of working together, Brian

to catch one's breath — *hier:* den Atem anhalten

had never used this signal. Abigail thought quickly. Should she call for a team of police officers to come immediately? Or should she first check and see if something was really wrong? After all, Brian was getting older. Maybe he had just been a bit careless.

Abigail decided to investigate the situation first. She quickly got out of the car and went across the street to the pub's entrance. First she put her face to the small window in the door and tried to look inside. But it was too dark to see anything. She listened carefully, but there were no sounds coming from the pub. Then she tried the door. It was unlocked and Abigail pushed it open. She put her head through the door and called out Brian's name. There was no answer.

Abigail then felt around on the wall next to the door for the light switch. When her fingers found it, she turned on the lights.

What she saw made her raise a hand to her mouth to stop herself from screaming. There was a pool of blood on the floor right in front of her feet. What looked like a very dead Chinese man was lying right in the middle of it. Abigail knew immediately that there was no point checking to see if the man was still alive. There was just too much blood. But perhaps out of habit she bent down and pressed two fingers to his neck anyway. The body was still warm, but she couldn't feel a pulse. All she could do for the dead man now was try and find out who had killed him – and why.

Automatically, she reached for her phone and made three calls. The first was to police **headquarters** to report the crime and ask for **back-up**. The second one was to Inspector Shane Cooper. He wasn't working tonight, but he **was on call**. Abigail needed his help and experience. Cooper was the third member of the PSNI who knew about Buckles. He didn't answer the phone, though. She wondered where he was and then placed her third call, this one to Bowles.

headquarters	*hier:* Präsidium
back-up	Unterstützung
to be on call	Bereitschafts-dienst haben

Exercise 5: True or false? Markieren Sie mit richtig ✓ oder falsch – !

1. Abigail had problems finding a parking place. ☐

2. Brian had often used the sign to ask for help. ☐

3. Abigail knew straight away that the Chinese man was dead. ☐

4. Abigail was surprised that Cooper didn't answer his phone. ☐

After Superintendent Collins had left the reception, Bowles was very busy. He moved around the Great Hall and tried to listen to the conversations between the locals and the visiting Chinese. He was hoping to hear or see something that could give the police a clue about the selling – and buying – of business secrets in Belfast. So far, he hadn't found out anything useful. But there was Tamsin O'Reilly again. She was still talking to the same Chinese man, but she didn't look as pretty as before. Her face was very red and she seemed angry. Her voice was getting louder. Bowles decided to get a bit closer and just managed to catch a few words.

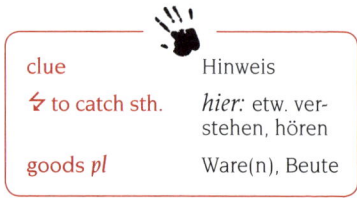

clue	Hinweis
↯ to catch sth.	*hier:* etw. verstehen, hören
goods *pl*	Ware(n), Beute

"This is not the right place, Mr Wu. You will get the goods tomorrow. I promise."

Bowles wondered what she meant by "goods". It sounded a little bit **suspicious**. He tried to hear more. The Chinese man, Mr Wu, was saying something about a "woman causing problems".

Unfortunately, just then Bowles' phone started ringing. It was really bad timing. Tamsin O'Reilly heard it, looked around and noticed Bowles standing nearby. She quickly started saying something about the rainy weather.

"Damned mobile phones," Bowles **cursed**. Then he looked at the screen to see who was calling. It was Superintendent Collins.

suspicious	verdächtig
to curse	fluchen
self-defence	Selbstverteidigung

"Bowles, I need you to stop what you're doing and come to 'Buckley's' in Tomb Street right away."

"But, Superintendent, I'm…"

She didn't let him finish his sentence.

"I don't have time to explain everything now, Bowles. I've got a dead man here on the floor. And Brian Buckley is missing. For some reason, Cooper isn't answering his phone. So would you please try and reach him? I need you both here."

"Right. I'm on my way."

But Abigail didn't hear him. She had already hung up. So many questions were going through her head. Where was Brian? What was he involved in? And most importantly, was he safe?

Brian was lucky to be alive. The stranger had shot him in the left hand during the fight for the gun. The wound didn't hurt that much, but it was still bleeding. But that was nothing compared to the Chinese stranger's wounds. Brian was pretty sure his attacker was dead. He hadn't meant to kill him, but after Brian had got his other hand on the gun, the man had attacked again. That's when Brian had pulled the trigger in **self-defence**. The bullet had gone right through the man's heart.

Brian had then followed his instincts. And he was still following them. He put the end of his shirt on his bleeding hand and started walking faster. He was on his way to the Lagan Weir Lookout. With luck, he would find Cai there waiting for him. It was their agreed back-up meeting place, just in case anything ever went wrong. And tonight, things had gone wrong, really wrong. Brian was worried that Cai was in great danger. His eyes searched for any sign of her. His brain, though, was filled with pictures of what had just happened.

Exercise 6: Correct the mistakes. Lesen Sie weiter und korrigieren Sie die sechs Fehler im folgenden Absatz!

After he had shot the chinese man, Brian has turned off the lights in the pub and run inside. She'd been just in time to saw Cai run around the corner. And he had seen anybody following her.

1. _____
2. _____
3. _____
4. _____
5. _____
6. _____

Brian had wanted to go after them, but then a car had come around the corner. Abigail! That thought had made him nervous. So he'd hid behind a rubbish bin next door to the pub. He hadn't wanted Abigail to see him. He just wasn't sure if he could trust her. After all, the Chinese man had known that Brian was a spy. That meant someone with the PSNI or the Security Service had blown his cover. It could even be Abigail. So Brian had waited until she was inside the pub, then he'd started off after Cai. He was almost at the river now. There was still no sign of her. But he could hear something, a faint click, click, click coming from somewhere nearby. Brian recognized the sound of high-heeled shoes hitting the pavement. Please let it be her, he thought and began walking even faster towards the noise.

Cai was still running. But her feet were killing her and she was getting tired. She slowed down a little and took a look around her. She was near the docks on the Lagan River where the boat trips for tourists started. But at this time of night there weren't any tourists about. Cai had run this way instinctively. It was near her back-up meeting place with Brian. But would he come? What if he couldn't come? What if he were hurt, or even worse?

Those thoughts made Cai even more afraid. She didn't feel like waiting around in the rain and the dark. Maybe she should try and call Brian? She took out her elegant mobile phone. It had been a present from her father. He hadn't been able to give it to her in person. Instead, he had sent it with

weir	Wehr, Stauanlage
to trust	vertrauen
spy	Spion
to blow sb.'s cover	jmd. enttarnen
faint	schwach
in person	persönlich
to punch in	*hier:* eintippen

an expensive special delivery service from Hefei. That's where Cai had grown up and where her father still lived and worked.

Those thoughts reminded Cai of why she had started spying on her company all those months ago. But if things work out, she told herself, my father won't have to go back there. This was a happier thought and it gave Cai courage. She punched in Brian's number at the pub.

Hot Shots

Outside the pub, two **constables** were going from door to door. They were looking for **witnesses**. So far, no one they had talked to had seen or heard anything unusual. Inside, the pub was full of activity. Abigail watched the **evidence** technicians doing their

constable	Polizist
witness	Zeuge
evidence	Beweis
to dust for fingerprints	nach Fingerabdrücken untersuchen
coroner	Gerichtsmediziner

jobs. One of them was **dusting for fingerprints**. Another was taking photographs. The **coroner** was there and was just finishing her first examination of the body.

Exercise 7: Verb forms. Lesen Sie weiter und unterstreichen Sie die richtige Variante!

Chief Inspector Bowles **1.** was / had arrived and **2.** was / had trying to call Inspector Cooper again. He still **3.** wasn't / hadn't answering his phone. He also **4.** wasn't / hadn't replied to any of the text messages Bowles **5.** was / had sent.

This was another mystery to Abigail. And really, she felt, she **had enough on her plate** at the moment without having to worry about Cooper, too. There was still no clue about where Brian was. And the police also didn't know the dead man's name. The clothes he was wearing were very expensive, but his pockets were empty, except for a very high-tech smartphone. It wasn't switched on, though, and a police expert was busy trying to **crack** the password. Then maybe the police could use it to try and discover the man's identity – and how and why he had died.

"Well, Superintendent Collins," the coroner was saying, "I won't be able to tell you for sure until I do the autopsy. But it looks as if the man was killed **instantly**. One shot, right through the heart."

"The technicians have found signs that the **victim recently** fired a gun," Abigail told the coroner, "though we haven't found a weapon. Still, is there any chance that he killed himself?"

"I don't think so. The entry wound is wrong. I think somebody shot him. But as I said, I'll be able to tell you more tomorrow." The coroner looked at her watch. "I mean later today."

The telephone behind the bar suddenly started ringing. Its tone was very loud and unexpected. Everyone stopped what they were doing and stared at it. Inspector Bowles asked if he should answer it. But Abigail shook her head.

"I'll get it," she told him.

The phone rang once more. Then Abigail picked up the **receiver**.

⚡ to have enough on one's plate	genug am Hals haben
to crack	knacken
instantly	sofort
victim	Opfer
recently	kürzlich
receiver	*hier:* Telefonhörer

She didn't say anything, but waited to see if the other person would speak first. The person did. Abigail heard a woman's voice but couldn't understand a word. The woman on the phone was speaking in a foreign language. It sounded like Chinese. The woman also seemed a little bit hysterical.

Exercise 8: Unscramble the text. Lesen Sie weiter und bringen Sie den Dialog in die richtige Reihenfolge!

a) "Where is he? And who are you?" the woman asked.

b) "I'm sorry, but I'm afraid he's, um... he's not here right now. May I help you?"

c) "Brian." the woman answered. "Please let me speak to Brian Buckley."

d) "Madam," Abigail **interrupted** her. "I'm sorry, but I can't understand you. Do you speak English?"

1	2	3	4

Before Abigail could identify herself, the woman said something else. She sounded surprised – and frightened.

"What's that? Is someone... who's there?" she **gasped**. "Brian, is that you?"

It took Abigail a second to realize that the woman was talking to someone else.

Suddenly, the woman screamed. "Help! Brian, no, no!"

Then Abigail heard gun shots. The woman screamed again. Abigail couldn't believe what was happening.

"Madam, madam are you okay? Are you still there?"

The only reply was the sound of the phone at the other end hitting the

| to interrupt | unterbrechen |
| to gasp | hörbar einatmen, nach Luft schnappen |

ground. Then the connection was as dead as the man on the floor of the pub.

At first, everyone working on the case in the pub was quiet, too.

Then the questions started coming at Abigail from all directions.

to trace	zurückverfolgen
nightmare	Albtraum
to yawn	gähnen
to turn up	auftauchen
⚡ telly	Glotze

"Who in the world was that?" asked the coroner.

"Can we **trace** the call?" a technician wanted to know.

"Was Brian Buckley there? Did he shoot her?" That was Bowles. And he had another question: "What the bloody hell is going on?"

Abigail didn't like it when Bowles cursed. But in her heart, she felt like doing it, too. The whole investigation was turning into a **nightmare**, and Abigail suspected it was going to get worse.

"I don't have the answers to your questions right now," she told them. "But together, we are going to find them. Now get back to work here. As soon as you're finished, report back to me at headquarters. It's going to be a long night."

A few hours later, as the sun began to come up over Belfast, Abigail watched the sky lightening from her office window in the eastern part of the city. She **yawned** and then stretched her tired shoulders. Then she picked up the cup of now cold tea from her desk and left for the conference room. Chief Inspector Bowles was already there. And Inspector Shane Cooper had finally **turned up**. Both men looked up from the papers in front of them as Abigail came into the room.

"Ah, Inspector Cooper. How very kind of you to join us." Abigail's words were very polite but the tone of her voice told Cooper she was not happy with him.

"I'm terribly sorry, Superintendent. I, um, was at home and fell asleep in front of the **telly**. For some reason, I just didn't hear my phone. It won't happen again."

Exercise 9: Tenses. Setzen Sie die Verben in der korrekten Zeitform ein!

be | not have | think | need | drink

Abigail **1.** _____ this was a **lame excuse**. Cooper often **2.** _____ too much beer after work. Maybe he **3.** _____ at a pub again. But she **4.** _____ time now to question him about it. They **5.** _____ to discuss more important things.

"So, I want to know what you've learnt so far. Bowles, you start."
Bowles picked up one of the papers in front of him.
"Okay, we have finally identified the victim. His name is Chung Ming. He was 34 years old, married and had one child. He lives, I mean lived, in Belfast with his family. He was a well-paid computer programmer. But his wife told us he spent a lot of his money on **gambling**. We're looking into that."
"Do we have any idea what he was doing at the pub last night?"
"No, Superintendent. His wife reported him missing a couple of hours ago. We know that he was at the Lord Mayor's reception last night, but he left early."

"Have we had any luck cracking his smartphone?"
"Yes. And that's where things get really interesting. His call records were empty. But there was one text

| lame excuse | faule Ausrede |
| gambling | Glücksspiel |

message still in the file. It said 'Am taking care of the woman. You kill the spy'."

"The spy?" Abigail was shocked to hear this. "That must mean Brian! Who sent the message?"

"We don't know yet," Bowles answered. "But our expert is working on it. He's also still trying to get into Mr Chung's email account."

Cooper frowned at this news.

"Okay. Let's move on," Abigail told them. "What about the phone call from the unknown woman to the pub?"

Bowles looked down at another one of the papers.

"We've had no reports of an injured or dead woman. But a couple of people did hear gunshots late last night near the Lookout. Someone also saw a man running away from the area shortly after."

to frown	die Stirn runzeln
injured	verletzt
downside	Nachteil
⚡ to be up to sth.	etw. vorhaben

Inspector Cooper's frown deepened and he asked, "Could they describe the man?"

"Not really." Bowles replied. "It was too dark. But the caller said the man was tall and thin and wearing a dark hat."

"Then it wasn't Brian," said Abigail. "He's quite short and well, he's not exactly fat, but he's got a big beer belly."

"Yes, well, that's one of the downsides to working in a pub." Cooper laughed a little bit as he said this.

"This is no time for jokes, Cooper. Brian is in danger. It's our job to find him, not laugh about him."

"Well actually, Superintendent Collins, we don't really know what Brian is up to. Here are the facts. We found a dead man in his pub. Brian's missing. The woman on the phone shouted his name before you heard the gunshots. That all sounds very suspicious."

Cooper's words made Abigail angry.

"Are you trying to say that Brian is involved in something fishy? I can't believe that for a second. Brian had found out something."
"Yes, but what, and how?" asked Bowles. "And Superintendent Collins, I think I've found out something, too."

| ⚡ fishy | suspekt, verdächtig |
| to overhear | zufällig hören |

Bowles told the others about the conversation he had overheard between Tamsin O'Reilly and the Chinese guest, Mr Wu.

Abigail raised an eyebrow at his report. "Well, it sounds like one of us needs to have a talk with the lovely Ms O'Reilly. Bowles, I'm sure you won't mind doing that!"

Bowles smiled to himself. That job would be a pleasure.
"No, I don't mind at all. I can call her as soon as we finish here."
"Not so fast, Bowles," Abigail told him. "Our top priority is for us to find Brian before something bad happens to him, or anyone else."

Just then someone knocked on the conference door. A young female constable came in.

"Sorry to interrupt you, Superintendent, but I thought you should know immediately. A woman's body has just been

> ID ist die Abkürzung für **identification**. **Employee ID card** bedeutet hier „Mitarbeiterausweis".

found at the end of Riverside Walk near the Weir. There's a bullet wound between her eyes."

Abigail closed her own tired eyes for a moment. There was just no end to the bad news in this case.

"Is the victim Chinese?"
"No, Superintendent."

That surprised Abigail. She waited for the constable to continue.
"The woman was a natural blonde and had blue eyes. We found an evening bag near her body. Inside it was an employee ID ⓘ card from the Lord Mayor's Office. It belonged to Tamsin O'Reilly."

Exercise 10: Hidden words. Finden Sie zwölf Wörter, die mit Polizeiarbeit zu tun haben!

F	A	R	Q	L	W	O	T	N	X	I
I	N	V	E	S	T	I	G	A	T	E
N	D	I	Y	B	L	O	O	D	R	O
G	H	C	L	U	E	F	D	B	I	X
E	S	T	F	L	U	M	S	A	C	E
R	P	I	A	L	W	E	A	P	O	N
P	Y	M	J	E	I	Y	U	N	R	T
R	M	E	Z	T	T	O	T	W	O	K
I	B	A	R	S	N	T	O	Q	N	L
N	O	T	U	H	E	V	P	F	E	I
T	R	A	C	E	S	M	S	Y	R	S
S	G	C	T	L	S	I	Y	A	T	D

# 4 A Long Shot

The news of Tamsin O'Reilly's death shocked the visitors from Hefei. They still hadn't **got over** the report about Chung Ming, and now this! Two murder victims! And both of them had been at the reception last night! The visitors had lots to discuss as they waited for their tour of Stevens Engineering to begin. It should have started half an hour ago. Ms Zheng was supposed to show them around the company, but she hadn't arrived yet. That gave the guests even more to talk about. One of them, Mr Liu, was especially worried. He wanted to ask her boss if she had **called in sick**. But then Arthur Stevens began speaking to the group.

to get over sth.	mit etw. fertig werden, über etw. hinwegkommen
to call in sick	sich krank melden
to assure sb. of sth.	jdm. etw. zusichern
lockers *pl*	Schließfächer

"Ladies and gentlemen, may I have your attention please!"

The visitors all politely stopped talking and listened to the company owner's words.

"I know you are all sad and sorry about the horrible deaths of Ms O'Reilly and Mr Chung. But I can **assure** you, our Police Service is working very hard to solve the crimes. Now, if you will come with me, we'll begin our tour. The first stop is at the security desk."

Here, each guest had to put their bags, coats and other personal items in special **lockers**. Mr Stevens explained quickly that they couldn't take any cameras or mobiles inside the building's secure areas.

"These days, we have to be very careful. As you all know, business in Belfast has grown enormously in the past years. But unfortunately it has also made us a **target** for industrial crimes."

"What kind of crimes?" one of the guests asked him.

"Well, um…"

Arthur Stevens wasn't quite sure how to answer tactfully.

"I mean, for example, stealing plans for new products or lists of customer contacts and then selling them to the **competition**."

None of the guests seemed **offended**, so Mr Stevens continued.

target	Ziel
competition	*hier:* Konkurrenz
to be offended	beleidigt sein

Exercise 11: Adjective or Adverb? Ergänzen Sie die Sätze mit der richtigen Form der angegebenen Begriffe!

`true` `slight` `serious` `loud` `possible` `secret`

"That's why security is a top priority and we take it very **1. _____**. Here at Stevens Engineering, we are doing everything **2. _____** to keep our business secrets exactly that – **3. _____**."

Most of the guests smiled **4. _____**. And several of them even clapped their hands **5. _____**. But two of them knew very well that the last sentence just was not **6. _____**.

It can't be true, Abigail thought as she finished buttoning her blouse. She was still at headquarters. There hadn't been time to go home yet. Luckily, she always kept clean clothes in the office. She felt much better now that she had on a fresh uniform. She quickly combed her short brown hair and then sat down in front of her computer. After she had switched it on, her thoughts turned back to the case.

standard operating procedure	übliches Vorgehen
re:	AW: (E-Mail)
to decipher	entschlüsseln

No, she didn't believe it. Brian Buckley would never, ever join the bad guys. Cooper must be crazy to think such a thing. Still, it was very strange that Brian had not tried to contact her. That was **standard operating procedure** in the world of spies. Brian knew that. So why was he breaking this important rule? Abigail hoped he had a very good reason. She didn't want to think about the alternatives. Maybe Brian was hurt – or dead and couldn't contact her.

The computer was online now and Abigail checked her mails. As usual, there were lots of them. But Abigail clicked past them quickly. She was looking for a special name. Brian was not a big internet user. He didn't trust it. He liked to use old-fashioned ways of communication. But Abigail had made him promise to use email in case of an emergency. Together they had worked out a simple code. And bingo! There it was, a message from "Mary". The "**re:**" line said "thank you for the flowers".

Abigail was so happy to see it that she almost laughed out loud. "Mary" was the code word Brian used to inform Abigail that he was alive and okay. The flowers part meant Brian needed to see her. She opened the mail and read the short message. It was also written in code, but Abigail was quickly able to **decipher** the message. Brian wanted to meet her at 1:00 p.m. in the Crown Liquor Saloon. She should come alone and not tell anyone else that he had contacted her.

Abigail looked at her watch. She still had a couple of hours left before the meeting. She wondered why Brian didn't want anyone else to know about it. She leaned back in her chair and put her feet on the desk. Slowly she began going over the facts in this puzzling case once more.

Exercise 12: Fill in the blanks. Vervollständigen Sie die Definitionen mit Vokabeln aus dem Text!

1. Something that is very important has top _____ _____.

2. If you say something rude or personal to someone, they could be _____.

3. If you have lots of options, you have many _____ _____.

4. If you believe in someone, you _____ them.

Months ago, her team had started looking into industrial espionage in Belfast. Luckily, the Lord Mayor and the City Council were helping with the investigation. After all, it was costing the city a lot of money. But Abigail's team wasn't very interested in who was buying business secrets. They were looking for the "insiders". Industrial espionage couldn't be successful without them. Typically, these people were company employees, and they sold the secrets they stole to a competing business. In these days of globalization, the buyers could be anywhere. So far, the investigation had been a **dead end**. But maybe now Brian was about to give her the missing piece that could solve the case. But why did he want to meet at the Crown? Wasn't that where…?

"Where did you say we are having lunch?" Mr Wu asked the woman standing next to him in front of the lockers. The tour of Stevens' Engineering had been very interesting indeed. But now, Mr Wu was hungry. He was also **impatient**. There was still no sign of Ms Zheng. And he was very worried about the fact that Tamsin O'Reilly was dead, too. How was he going to get the information now?

dead end	Sackgasse
impatient	ungeduldig
honoured	geehrt

"Good afternoon, everyone. I'm terribly sorry I'm late."
Zheng Cai's sudden appearance surprised everyone.
"Why Cai, where have you been? I was starting to think something had happened to you. It's not like you to be late."
"I really am very sorry, Mr Stevens. I'll, um, explain later," she told him and looked around at the Chinese visitors.
Arthur Stevens understood that Cai didn't want to discuss the issue in front of the **honoured** guests.
"Well, it's lovely, just lovely that you are here now to go with us for lunch at the Crown Liquor Saloon."
"Yes it is, isn't it? The Crown is one of Northern Ireland's most famous pubs. I love it there!" Cai smiled happily at the visitors. "I'm certain you are going to enjoy it, too. Shall we go?"
The group members all finished getting their things out of the lockers. Then they went outside to the waiting taxis. Mr Wu made sure to get inside the same one as Zheng Cai. He wasn't sure what was going on, but he was going to keep a close eye on her. For a couple of seconds, they were alone in the back of the taxi.
"Ms Zheng, have we still got a deal?" Mr Wu whispered.

"Of course we have, Mr Wu." Cai's voice shook a little.

"The unfortunate Ms O'Reilly told me you were causing problems. In fact, she said you…"

The taxi door suddenly opened. It was Mr Liu.

"Oh fine, there's still a free seat for me," he said and smiled kindly at Cai. "I'm very glad to see you looking so well, Ms Zheng."

"It's nice to see you again, too, Mr Liu." Then the taxi began the drive across the city to the beautiful, historic pub in Great Victoria Street.

unfortunate	*hier:* bedauernswert
to stand out	sich abheben
exterior	Außenseite
splendid	prächtig, grandios
stake-out	Observierung

The entrance to the Crown was across the street from the Great Northern Mall. That's where Brian Buckley was standing. It was a very busy place. The Europa Bus Centre was also nearby. Brian had on comfortable travelling clothes and was carrying a small overnight bag. Nothing about the way he looked made him stand out from the other people around.

Exercise 13: Choose the correct alternative. Lesen Sie weiter und unterstreichen Sie die richtige Variante!

He 1. had / was having a Belfast guide book open in his hand, but he 2. didn't read / wasn't reading it. Brian 3. looked / was looking at the colourful exterior of the Crown. But it wasn't the splendid architecture he 4. admired / was admiring . For the first time in years, Brian 5. ran / was running a stake-out.

It was just like back in the old days. The trick was to **take in** every detail and to make sure that nobody noticed you doing it. To be honest[i], Brian really didn't miss that part of spying. In fact, he was starting to think that he was getting too old for the spy business. Maybe he should think about **retirement**. Just then he **spotted** a woman coming up to the Crown's entrance. It was Abigail, and

To be honest bedeutet hier „ehrlich gesagt" und wird im umgangssprachlichen Englisch sehr häufig benutzt.

she seemed to be alone. He watched her go through the pub's doors, but he didn't follow her. He was waiting for another familiar face to turn up. And just two minutes later, it did. But it wasn't the person Brian had thought would follow Abigail to the Crown. Brian was very disappointed and sad to see who was trying to look through the Crown's front window. But he couldn't feel bad about it now. It was time to **take his long shot**. Hopefully, Abigail and Cai would both do their part.

Abigail went inside the Crown and looked around for Brian. She didn't see him. A waiter came up to her immediately.
"Excuse me, **ma'am**. Are you Superintendent Collins?"
Abigail tried not to show her surprise.
"This is for you, Superintendent. I'm to tell you it's from Mary."
The waiter handed her an envelope. Then he told her to please have a seat in one of the Crown's ten wooden **booths**. These were called snugs. They were a special feature in many old pubs. Originally, the snugs were used by people who wanted to have a drink in private. It was the perfect place for a secret meeting. After the waiter left, Abigail opened and read the message that was really from Brian.
It took her breath away.

to take in	aufnehmen; begreifen
retirement	Ruhestand
to spot sb.	jmd. sehen
⚡ to take a long shot	etw. ergebnislos versuchen
ma'am	Abk. Madam, gnädige Frau
booth	*hier:* Separee

 Last Shot

Abigail read the shocking message again. "Abigail! Someone else on our team has followed you to the Crown. I'm sure they are being paid to work for the other side!"

traitor	Verräter
to treat one-self to sth.	sich etw. gönnen
to disturb	stören

Abigail stopped reading. That meant there was a traitor at PSNI! The rest of the message had clear instructions for Abigail.

"When the person arrives, act surprised to see them! Invite them to sit with you. Don't let them leave! Trust me, I have a plan!"

Abigail folded the message and quickly put it in her pocket. She put her head out of the snug a bit so she could see the entrance.

She was still trying to take in what Brian had written. Then she saw him. Inspector Shane Cooper was coming through the doors. Abigail put a fake smile on her face and waved at Cooper. He waved back and started coming towards her.

"Hello, Superintendent Collins. What brings you here?"

Cooper was trying to act surprised. Abigail knew that he wasn't.

"Oh, I decided to treat myself to a nice lunch," she lied. "I needed a break from the office and the case."

"Are you expecting anyone?"

"Oh no," she said. "Um, why don't you join me?"

"Well, if you're sure I'm not disturbing you, I'd be glad to."

Cooper sat down across from her. Abigail kept Brian's instructions in mind.

"And you, Inspector Cooper, what are you doing here? The Crown is quite a distance from headquarters."

"Oh, I wanted to have a look around the Bus Centre. See if anyone there remembers seeing Brian. Maybe he's left the city."

Cooper really did **have a nerve**!

Exercise 14: Verb forms. Lesen Sie weiter und setzen Sie die Verben in der korrekten Zeitform ein!

| want | ring | try | come | ask | say |

Abigail **1.** _____ to stay calm. To **buy some time**, she **2.** _____ Cooper if he **3.** _____ something to eat or drink. He **4.** _____ yes and Abigail **5.** _____ a little bell in the snug to call the waiter. He **6.** _____ over almost at once to take their orders.

"I'll have a pot of tea and a **pasty**," Abigail told him.

"And you, sir?"

"The same for me," Cooper answered. When the waiter left, Abigail took a deep breath.

⚡ to have a nerve	die Dreistigkeit besitzen
to buy some time	etw. Zeit gewinnen
pasty	Pastete

"So you really do think that Brian has something to hide?"

"I'm just trying to keep an open mind, Sir. But if Brian Buckley is one hundred per cent honest, why hasn't he got in touch with us?"

Cooper stopped talking and bent his head down so he could look her directly in the eyes. "Or has he?"

Abigail had had enough of Cooper's game.

"Has he what, Cooper? Has he contacted me? Has he left town? Has he murdered two people? You tell me!"

Cooper didn't answer. He just looked at her strangely. Abigail realized she had said too much. It was a good thing that the waiter came back just then with their tea and pasties. It gave her a moment to calm down.

"Sorry Cooper, for exploding like that. I'm afraid this entire case has too many questions and not enough answers."

"Well, Superintendent, I think Cooper has answers for you!"

to arrest	festnehmen
handcuffs *pl*	Handschellen
to lunge	losstürzen
to grab	greifen, schnappen

It was Brian! He'd appeared as if by magic at their booth.

"What do you mean by that, Buckley?" Cooper started to get up from the table.

"You know very well what I mean, Cooper! You've been taking money in exchange for..."

"That's enough, Buckley! I'm **arresting** you for the murders of Chung Ming and Tamsin O'Reilly!"

Cooper was now on his feet and reaching for his **handcuffs**.

In that moment, Arthur Stevens, Cai and the group of visitors from Hefei came into the Crown. Cai was leading them. When she saw Cooper, she stopped dead and pointed her finger at him.

"That's him. That's the man who tried to shoot me last night."

"That's a lie! Brian Buckley attacked you. I saw him do it."

Cooper **lunged** for Brian and **grabbed** one of his arms.

Abigail knew she had to get control of the situation.

"Cooper stop it, let him go," she ordered.

But Cooper was desperate now. He had one hand on Brian. With the other, he pulled out a gun.

Abigail grabbed the pot of tea and threw the hot liquid at Cooper. He screamed and let go of Brian. But he didn't drop the weapon.
The Chinese guests didn't know what to think about this scene. Some of them thought it was some kind of entertainment and began to laugh and applaud. Mr Wu wasn't laughing. He knew **the game was up** and started to back slowly towards the door.

the game is up	das Spiel ist aus

Cooper saw him trying to escape and pointed his gun at Mr Wu. "Not so fast! If I'm going down, I'm taking you with me!"
He pulled back the gun's trigger and fired. The bullet hit Mr Wu in the shoulder. Then a second bullet raced through the air. But this one came from another gun. Chaos broke out in the Crown. People were screaming and trying to find a place to hide from the gunfire. Brian was holding the weapon he had taken from Mr Chung. He had just fired at Cooper's arm. But he had missed. He fired again. It was the last bullet in the gun and this time, it hit the target. The bullet hit Cooper right between the eyes and he fell to the floor. The traitor was dead.

Exercise 15: Definitions. Ordnen Sie die passende Definition zu!

1. ☐ be honest   a) see
2. ☐ have something to hide   b) have a secret
3. ☐ to treat oneself   c) tell the truth
4. ☐ to spot   d) do something nice for yourself

Blood was pouring from Mr Wu's shoulder, but he still kept moving towards the door.

"Stop him," Brian shouted.

Abigail started towards Mr Wu, but Mr Liu was faster. The small Chinese man turned into a fighting machine. He kicked Mr Wu in the stomach and knocked him down. A quick punch to the wounded shoulder took care of the rest. Mr Wu wouldn't be going anywhere now.

to bow	sich verbeugen
(to put) first things first	eins nach dem anderen (machen)
Sláinte *IRL*	Prost (gälisch)

Mr Liu turned around and **bowed** to the people watching from their hiding places. None of them could believe what they had just witnessed. Cai was the first one to speak.

"Father, you were simply wonderful! I didn't know that you were still such a good fighter."

"Well, Cai, children never do know everything about their parents, do they?" Mr Liu smiled at his daughter and then he looked at Brian.

"Ah, Buckles, old man. It's just like the good old days, isn't it?"

That was one surprise too many for Abigail.

"Brian, what exactly is going on here?"

"**First things first**, Superintendent. There'll be time for explanations later. We need to call for an ambulance and back-up. And I don't know about the rest of you, but I need a drink."

Brian looked at the shocked man standing behind the bar.

"Barkeeper, how about a round for everyone?"

"Cheers."

"**Sláinte**."

The small group of people sitting around a table at "Buckley's" all raised their glasses. Brian, Abigail, Bowles, Cai and Mr Liu were all drinking whiskey . They were tired, but very happy. Abigail had the answers to most of her questions.

> Neben dem beliebten Dunkelbier *Guinness* ist Whiskey eines der beliebtesten Getränke der Iren.

She now knew that Tamsin O'Reilly, Shane Cooper and Chung Ming had all secretly worked for Mr Wu. He was the mastermind behind the industrial espionage. Tamsin had kept him up-to-date about local busi-

mastermind	Drahtzieher, führender Kopf
to bribe	bestechen
to threaten	bedrohen

nesses that could have interesting secrets. Her position at the Lord Mayor's office had been very helpful. Then she and Chung had looked for potential insiders. These employees were either bribed or threatened to steal secrets from their employers. That had mostly been Chung's job. Abigail could almost understand that Tamsin and Chung had done it for the money Mr Wu had paid them. But Cooper's part in the espionage ring was hard to believe.

Exercise 16: Pronouns. Lesen Sie weiter und setzen Sie die fehlenden Pronomen ein!

| she | her | He | him | his | himself |

1. _____ had been working for Mr Wu. Cooper had taken 2. _____ money and kept 3. _____ informed about the investigation. Cooper had found out about Brian and Cai. He knew 4. _____ was meeting with Brian. That's why Cooper had ordered Chung to kill Brian. He was going to take care of Cai 5. _____, but Brian had rescued 6. _____ in time.

Tamsin O'Reilly hadn't been so lucky. The police were almost certain that Cooper had killed her. The bullet in her head was from his gun. The police still weren't sure why Cooper had shot her. But Abigail suspected that Tamsin had panicked after she learnt about Chung's death and Cai's escape. Tamsin probably realized that the game was up. Perhaps she had even tried to blackmail Cooper. But that was still speculation and under investigation. As for Mr Wu, he was in hospital. He wasn't talking to the police.

"Cai, what I don't know is how you got involved in the first place?" Abigail asked.

"It was Chung Ming, Inspector Collins. He threatened me. He told me if I didn't steal secrets from Stevens Engineering, something very bad would happen to my father. So I did it."

Mr Liu continued the story. "When I talked to my daughter on the phone, I realized something was wrong. I called Brian and asked him to try and find out what it was. We go back a long way."

"And exactly how do you two know each other?" Cai asked.

"I can't tell you that, Cai," her father said. "It's top secret. Let's just say there's more than one old spy sitting at this table!"

to blackmail	erpressen
⚡ to go back a long way	sich schon lange kennen
⚡ shot for the road	Absacker

The other "old spy" laughed at this.

Then Brian explained how he had contacted Cai and convinced her to let him help her.

Abigail knew there were still many things to clear up. But she decided she had had just about enough for one day.

"Brian, I'll have another shot for the road."

He picked up the whiskey bottle and re-filled all their glasses.

"You can all be sure of one thing. 'Buckles' is retiring. I've fired my last shot from a gun. From now on, I'm only going to pour shots – and drink them. Sláinte!"

Waving Death

Gina Billy

 Making Waves

Another big wave **rocked** the car ferry and sent salty water flying into Phoebe Calloway's face. She smiled to herself as she licked the drops from her lips. They tasted like home. Oh it felt so good to be coming back to the Isle of Wight! That's where Phoebe had grown up. But her father had got a job in London when Phoebe was sixteen and her family had then moved to the **mainland**. Now she was almost thirty.

to rock	schaukeln
mainland	Festland
strait	Meeresstraße
frown	Stirnrunzeln

This was her first trip back to the island in all those years. In just ten more minutes, the voyage from Southampton across the Sorent **Strait** would be over.

It was warm outside on the ship's deck, but the sky was starting to get cloudy. It was still clear enough, though, for Phoebe to see East Cowes getting closer. The town's name was pronounced like "cows", but there weren't any around. Instead, the harbour was filled with all kinds of boats. Phoebe's smile got bigger. Hopefully, she would have time to do some sailing. The wind suddenly blew her long, dark brown hair in front of her eyes. Phoebe pushed it back and her smile changed to a **frown**. She reminded herself that she was not on holiday. She was returning to the island because of work. The job she had been given to do was hard, dangerous and above all – secret.

Captain Manuel Rodriquez couldn't help worrying about the cargo hidden in the yacht's **hold**. So far, it had been **smooth sailing** for him and the five crew members on board the expensive boat. They had left their home port in South America last week and enjoyed eight days of excellent weather. But now, the waves on the open sea were getting higher and higher. The wind was also blowing stronger and Captain Rodriguez was worried. A storm was coming. And his seaman's instincts told him it was going to be a bad one. The "Blues" was a fine ship, though, and she should manage the storm without too many problems. No, the trouble was his cargo. It had to be at the Isle of Wight at midnight in just two days. The storm could make him miss that deadline. That would make his contact on the island very unhappy. And being late would also cost Captain Rodriguez and his crew a very **fat cash bonus**. Even worse, the "Blues" was not on the way to a safe harbour. Instead, she was sailing to the island's southern coast. The water there was filled with rocks and well-known for **shipwrecks**. Rodriguez cursed in Spanish. If the "Blues" did get into trouble, he could not call the coastguard for help. It would **make a lot of waves** if police found his cargo.

hold	*hier:* Frachtraum
smooth sailing	*hier:* ruhige Fahrt
fat cash bonus	fette Barprämie
shipwreck	Schiffsunglück
to make a lot of waves	großen Aufruhr verursachen
manor	Herrenhaus
to keep in touch	in Kontakt bleiben

None of the people Phoebe knew on the island must know the real reason for her visit. That was going to be hard, especially at Bainbridge **Manor**. That's where Phoebe was going to stay. Alec Bainbridge was an old friend of her father's; the two men had **kept in touch** for years. Alec and his second wife Maura had often invited Phoebe to visit. Still, Alec had been sur-

hospitality	Gastfreundlichkeit
to put a stop to sth.	einer Sache ein Ende machen

prised when Phoebe had called two days ago to ask if she could come and stay for a few days. He had said, yes, of course. Phoebe felt a little bit bad about accepting the Bainbridge's hospitality. But her boss had told her that the Bainbridge family home was the perfect location for Phoebe to do the job in front of her. And maybe Alec and his sons, Jordan and Trent, could help her.

Exercise 1: Adverbs. Lesen Sie weiter und unterstreichen Sie die richtige Variante!

The thought of Jordan Bainbridge made Phoebe's heart beat a **1.** little / few faster. He had been **2.** so / such a good looking boy! Phoebe wondered what he looked like **3.** yet / now . The two of them had played a **4.** lot / lots together as children. **5.** Then / When they were teenagers, their feelings for **6.** every / each other had started to change.

Jordan had even kissed her once! But Phoebe's move to London had put a stop to their innocent romance.
"Ladies and Gentlemen, please prepare for arrival."
The message from the ship's captain made Phoebe stop thinking about the past. It was time to get to work and follow orders.

"What time is Phoebe arriving?" Jordan Bainbridge asked his father. The two of them were sitting on the terrace at Bainbridge Manor.

The lovely old house was just outside Ventnor. The terrace and gardens had a beautiful view over Monks **Bay** and they could hear the waves **crashing** on the rocks below.

"She should be here in time for drinks before dinner," his father Alec replied. "Maura's also invited a few other people. Are you nervous about seeing Phoebe again?"

"No, not really. It's just a bit strange to think about her coming back to visit after all this time."

Alec also thought that Phoebe's spontaneous visit was a bit surprising. It also wasn't the best time for her to come. He **had a lot on his mind** at the moment and wasn't really in the mood for guests.

bay	Bucht
to crash	*hier:* brechen
to have a lot on one's mind	den Kopf voll haben
to be back on one's feet	wieder auf die Füße kommen
to get re-acquainted with sb.	jmd. wieder besser kennenlernen
customs *pl*	Zoll
dreadfully	schrecklich

There were so many problems. His marriage to Maura was in trouble. His youngest son, Trent, was being very difficult – again. The family's shipbuilding business still wasn't **back on its feet** after the financial crisis. But most of all, Alec was very worried about what was going to happen two days from now.

"Dad?"

Alec realized Jordan was waiting for him to say something.

"Well, Jordan, I'm sure you and Phoebe will enjoy **getting re-acquainted**. She was always a lovely girl."

"Did she say why she suddenly decided to come?"

"Well, just that work was a bit slow at the moment and that her boss had given her a few days off."

"What does she do?"

"She didn't say much about it. Something about 'import and export' in a London company and '**customs** and tax paperwork'."

"How **dreadfully** boring," a woman's voice said.

Maura Bainbridge was coming through the glass doors with a gin and tonic in her hand. It wasn't her first drink of the day. She **stumbled** slightly and **spilt** part of her drink on her short, red dress. As usual, Alec didn't comment on his wife's alcohol problem.
"Maura, darling, you look beautiful. I love it when you wear red. It is a wonderful colour on you," he said and stood up to kiss her.
But Maura turned her lips away from him.
"Well, well Jordan. I see you've come home from the **shipyards** early. Can't you wait to see your old flame?"
Maura was already so drunk that it was hard to understand what she was saying. But her sarcastic tone made it clear that she wasn't being nice to him. That was usual, too.

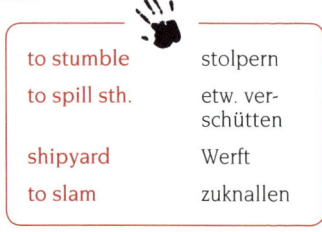

to stumble	stolpern
to spill sth.	etw. verschütten
shipyard	Werft
to slam	zuknallen

Exercise 2: Odd one out. Welches Wort ist das „schwarze Schaf"? Unterstreichen Sie!

1. son   husband   man   brother

2. kind   lovely   wonderful   beautiful

3. employer   boss   supervisor   chef

4. difficult   trouble   problem   worry

Jordan started to say something unpleasant to her, but then he heard the sound of a car speeding up the drive. It wasn't Phoebe, though. The silver sports car belonged to his younger brother. The group on the terrace watched Trent Bainbridge park the car, open the door and **slam** it shut.

"What's the matter with Trent?" Maura asked her husband.

"Oh, it's nothing important dear. The two of us had a little talk at work this morning, there's no need for you to worry."

Jordan could only shake his head at his father. The "little talk" had been a very big fight. Everyone in the office at the shipyards had heard Trent and their father shouting at each other. Clearly, Trent was still angry. Just then he came up to the others.

"Hello Maura, Jordan." After a slight pause he added, "Dad."

Then he saw Maura's almost empty glass.

"Would you like another, Maura? I could use one, too. It hasn't been a great day."

Maura smiled at Trent and started to give him her glass. Before he could take it, Alec took it gently out of her hand.

"Maura's waiting until Phoebe arrives, Trent. She should be here any time now."

Area of Outstanding Beauty	Region von herausragender Schönheit, Naturpark
cliff	Klippe
cove	Bucht
United Kingdom Border Agency	brit. Grenzschutzorganisation

Phoebe stopped her car just a few miles away from Bainbridge Manor to take a short break. She had really enjoyed the drive right through the middle of the diamond-shaped island. The Isle of Wight covered an area of 147 square miles. That made it the largest island in England. Almost half of it was an official "Area of Outstanding Beauty". The landscape included rivers, forests, farm land, sandy beaches and incredible sandstone and chalk cliffs. There were also hidden coves and high points looking out over the English Channel. These had often been used in the past by pirates and smugglers.

Phoebe was very afraid that the island was still a smuggler's paradise. She took out a piece of paper from her handbag. It was a copy of a letter sent to her boss at the United Kingdom Border Agency last week. It said, "Large shipment cocaine arriving by ship. Midnight, April 28th, near Ventnor. Local boats involved."

law enforcement force	Strafverfolgungsbehörde
to investigate	untersuchen, ermitteln
suspect	Verdächtiger

The Agency was one of the United Kingdom's largest law enforcement forces. One of its jobs was to patrol the United Kingdom's borders. It often got information about drug smuggling from people who didn't give their names. Phoebe was a Specialist Detective with the Agency's Border Force. Its director, David Sims, had given her the job of investigating the anonymous tip.

Director Sims knew that Phoebe had grown up on the island. So he had sent her back here undercover. She was to talk to the locals and learn as much as she could. She was also going to look at places near Ventnor where smugglers could bring in their cargo. April 28th was just two days away. There wasn't much time left to look for suspects. Phoebe sent a quick text message to her boss to say that she had arrived. Then she got back in the car. Alec's business was sailors and ships. Phoebe was about to make it police business to find out if he knew something that could help her.

Exercise 3: Verb forms. Ergänzen Sie Simple Past und Past Participle der folgenden Verben!

1. give _____ _____

2. go _____ _____

3. find _____ _____

4. make _____ _____

Waves of Suspicion

"So tell me, Alec. How are things in the Bainbridge shipyards?" Phoebe asked and took another sip of white wine.

"Well, I'm afraid that business isn't so good right now. The financial crisis has hit us hard. Lots of people just don't have the money to buy our boats at the moment. But I hope the new prototype Jordan designed will change that."

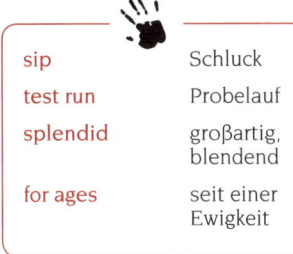

sip	Schluck
test run	Probelauf
splendid	großartig, blendend
for ages	seit einer Ewigkeit

Alec was sitting at the head of the oval dining room in Bainbridge Manor. Phoebe was seated next to him. So far, the evening had gone well. The Bainbridge's and their two other dinner guests had made Phoebe feel welcome. There had been a lot of small talk during the meal. But now, they were finished eating and Phoebe had turned the conversation around to business.

Mit dem Begriff **Manor** bezeichnet man in Großbritannien ein Landgut oder ein Herrenhaus.

"Yes, Phoebe. Our new sailing yacht is very innovative. As long as the weather doesn't get any worse, Jordan's taking it out for a test run tomorrow morning. Jordan, why don't you take Phoebe with you?"

Jordan looked across the table at Phoebe.

"What a splendid idea," he said. "Do you want to come, Phoebe?"

"Oh, that would be lovely! I haven't been sailing for ages."

Exercise 4: Adjectives. Lesen Sie weiter und unterstreichen Sie im folgenden Absatz alle sechs Adjektive!

How perfect, Phoebe thought. It would give her a great chance to have a closer look at the interesting coast near Ventnor. And she could use the time alone with Jordan to **fish for information**. Besides that, she could even **combine business with pleasure**. Jordan had grown up to be a very attractive man.

"Can I come along with you?" asked Trent.
He hadn't spoken much to anyone except Maura during the meal. But he'd been busy keeping her glass filled with red wine.
"Certainly not, young man," Alec told him. "I need you in the office first thing tomorrow morning. I'm still waiting for your written report about how things went in South America."
"Well, Dad, I tried to tell you this morning, but you wouldn't let me. Things went okay. I had a lot of good meetings, especially in Columbia. But nothing is **written in stone** yet. I'm sure we'll find some buyers there, though."
"Maybe I can help you out there, Trent," said the woman sitting at Trent's right.
Zoe Allan was what people on the Isle of Wight called an "overner". That meant she lived on the island but hadn't been born there. She was a beautiful blonde in her late 30's.

to fish for information	*hier:* nach Informationen suchen
to combine business with pleasure	das Angenehme mit dem Nützlichen verbinden
to be written in stone	in Stein gemeißelt sein

"My ex-husband Tom and I do lots of business in South America. In fact, I was in Bogota last week. I have great contacts there."

"How interesting," Phoebe said. And it certainly was. Two of the people at the table had just returned from South America! Phoebe would be sure to mention that in her next report to Director Sims.

"And what kind of business are you in?" asked Phoebe.

line of business	Branche
shop talk	Fachsimpelei
to shatter	*hier:* zerbrechen
to pour	*hier:* fließen
⚡ to catch sth.	*hier:* etw. verstehen, hören
awkward	unangenehm, peinlich

Before Zoe could answer, the man sitting between Phoebe and Maura did it for her. Ethan Saunders owned another shipyard on the island. It had surprised Phoebe to see him here because Ethan and Alec were business rivals.

"Actually, Zoe and Tom, her ex, are sort of in the same **line of business** as I am. Oh, and Alec, too of course. The two of us build boats and Zoe uses them. She has a shipping company."

Phoebe wanted to ask more but didn't get the chance.

"I just can't hear any more of this **shop talk**," Maura said loudly.

Then she suddenly stood up and slammed her wine glass down on the table. The crystal glass **shattered** and cut her hand. Blood and red wine were **pouring** onto the white table cloth. Alec jumped up to go to the other end of the table and help her.

"No, Alec, don't touch me!" Maura practically shouted. "Trent, would you please help me to my room? I'm sorry, everyone, terribly sorry."

Trent got up and took Maura's arm. She looked as if she were about to cry. Trent led her from the room and spoke softly to her. Phoebe could hardly **catch** his words. But she managed to hear him say, "It will all be better soon, Maura, don't worry."

Then he closed the dining room door. There was an **awkward** silence. No one knew what to say. Alec was still standing next to

Maura's empty chair. It was Zoe who spoke first.

⚡ what's got into her — was ist mit ihr los

"Alec, dear, I'm feeling a bit tired. Would you mind very much if I left for home now?"

"Of course not, Zoe. I'm sorry about the scene. Maura, well, I don't know **what's got into her**. She hasn't been herself lately."

"Oh, really Dad! You know very well what's wrong with Maura!"

"Not now, Jordan! Listen, I'll just bring Zoe out to her car. Why don't you offer Phoebe and Ethan a brandy?"

"Not for me, Alec," said Ethan. "I've had enough. Just like Maura."

That remark was quite rude and Ethan realized his mistake.

"Actually Alec, I should be going as well. You can stay here. I'll be glad to walk with Zoe to her car."

Alec looked strangely disappointed. And Zoe didn't seem very happy about Ethan's offer, either. But there was no way for her to say no tactfully.

Exercise 5: Fill in the blanks. Lesen Sie weiter und setzen Sie die Wörter richtig ein!

| see | we | meet | us | everyone | each other |

"Well, thank you, Ethan, and good night 1._____.

Phoebe, it was nice to 2._____ you. I hope we

see 3._____ again before you leave."

"Yes, Phoebe, it was very nice to 4._____ you

again after all these years," Ethan said. "And Alec, thanks for

having 5._____. Zoe, shall 6._____?"

Ethan **motioned to** Zoe and they started to leave the room. Phoebe saw Alec watch them go. Funny, his eyes seemed to be very focused on Zoe's lovely legs.

"Um, I just remembered that I need to tell Zoe something," he said. "I'll, um, be right back."

Alec hurried after his departing guests and left Jordan and Phoebe alone.

"What an **awful** end to your first evening back, Phoebe. I'm sorry."

"Don't worry about it, Jordan. All families have problems. Do you want to talk about it?"

"That's kind of you, Phoebe, but no, not tonight. Maybe I'll feel like talking about it tomorrow. Now, how about that brandy?"

Part of Phoebe wanted to sit with Jordan over a **nightcap**. But the detective part of her had a lot to think about. There was also something she wanted to check on before making her next report.

"No thanks, Jordan. I think I'll go up to my room. It's been a long day. I'll see you early in the morning."

"All right, Phoebe. I'll just go to the kitchen and let the housekeeper know the party's over. But Phoebe," he added and looked at her with a smile in his eyes, "I just want you to know how glad I am that you are here. Good night."

"Me too, Jordan. And I'm really looking forward to our sailing trip. Good night and sleep well."

to motion to sb.	jmd. durch ein Zeichen auffordern
awful	schlimm, schrecklich
nightcap	Schlummertrunk

Phoebe walked quickly out of the room. But she didn't take the stairs up to the guest room on the first floor. She went quietly out of the front door. A loud wind was blowing now and clouds were covering the almost full moon. The outside lights were on, though, and Phoebe saw a car disappearing down the drive. A dark green Jaguar was parked on the other side of Trent's car. A man and a woman were standing very close to each other right beside it. It was Alec and Zoe. It didn't look like they were talking business. They hadn't seen Phoebe yet and she looked for a place where she could hide. A large, **leafy** plant was right next to the front door and Phoebe got behind it.

leafy	mit viel Grün, belaubt
on tiptoes	auf Zehenspitzen
passionate	leidenschaftlich
to slip out	herausschlüpfen
wickedly	böse

She was just in time. Alec looked up towards the house. Then he put his arms around Zoe. She stood up **on tiptoes** and raised her head. Then Alec bent towards her and their lips met in a **passionate** kiss.

Phoebe didn't need to see any more. She started **to slip out** from behind her hiding place and go back into the house. But the sound of the front door opening made her stay where she was.

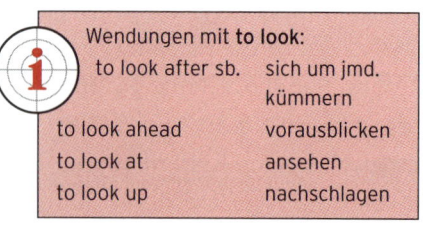

Wendungen mit **to look**:	
to look after sb.	sich um jmd. kümmern
to look ahead	vorausblicken
to look at	ansehen
to look up	nachschlagen

"Dad! When you finish kissing your lover, Maura wants to see you upstairs."

It was Trent. He laughed **wickedly** at the surprised look on his father's face.

"Oh, and Dad, make sure you're not wearing any of Zoe's lipstick. Maura is a drunk, but she's not stupid."

"Trent, wait! I can explain," Alec called to him.

But Trent just laughed his wicked laugh again and went back inside. Zoe said something to Alec that Phoebe couldn't hear. Then she touched Alec's cheek and got into the car. He watched her drive away. The sound of her car's motor grew quieter and quieter.

Then there was only the sound of the stormy wind and the nearby waves crashing on the shore. It was spooky, and for some reason, Phoebe felt afraid.

Suddenly, a bolt of lightning flashed across the sky followed by a loud clap of thunder. They startled Phoebe and she couldn't stop herself from letting out a little gasp of surprise. She hoped Alec hadn't heard her. His hearing was very good for a man of his age.

"What's that? Is someone there?" he called.

Alec started walking up the steps to the house. He was looking in Phoebe's direction and she almost stopped breathing. Surely, he would see her now! But then Alec shook his head and started talking to himself.

"Alec, old man," he said out loud. "This entire situation is really shattering your nerves. Now you're even hearing things!" Then he laughed strangely. "Or it's the Bainbridge Manor ghost again."

Phoebe let out a sigh of relief when Alec finally went back inside the house. Thank goodness he hadn't locked up behind him! Phoebe waited outside for a few minutes to make sure the coast was clear and to collect her thoughts. She had no idea what Alec had meant by the Bainbridge ghost. She was more interested in his "this situation" remark. Did he mean Maura's drinking and whatever was going on between him and Zoe? Or was something else worrying Alec? That was something she definitely would talk to Jordan about in the morning.

Phoebe suddenly realized how very tired she was. But she still had to send her report to Director Sims. It was time to go up to her guest room and finish her day's work. Then she could finally get some much needed sleep before the big day tomorrow.

shore	Küste
spooky	unheimlich
gasp of surprise	Laut des Erstaunens
sigh of relief	Seufzer der Erleichterung
the coast is clear	die Luft ist rein

Exercise 6: Reported speech. Fügen Sie die Wörter in der richtigen Reihenfolge hinzu, damit ein Satz in der indirekten Rede entsteht!

1. evening | first | Phoebe's | awful | was | back | really

   Jordan said _____

   _____

2. him | want | didn't | nightcap | have | a | to | she

   Phoebe told _____

   _____

3. upstairs | Maura | to | him | Alec | see | that | wanted

   Trent told _____

   _____

4. ghost | again | Manor | of | back | was | if | the | Bainbridge

   Alec wondered _____

   _____

3. Deadly Waves

The sun was just starting to come up and Maura still hadn't been to sleep. She was sitting at the antique writing desk in her room. She and Alec had had separate rooms for some time now. Maura looked down at what she had just written on her personal, light pink stationery. Then she looked out of the window and saw the first rays of the sun turn the cloudy sky red. Her head was aching from all the alcohol. The cut on her hand

| stationery | Briefpapier |
| ray | Strahl |

was hurting, too. But there were other problems that had kept her up all night. What was she going to do about Trent – and Alec? Maura decided to go outside and watch the sunrise. Maybe it would help her feel better. She was still wearing the dress she'd had on at dinner.

She put on a pair of flat shoes and got a raincoat out of her dressing room. Then she went out of the veranda doors and walked to the end of the garden. A path there led along the cliffs that fell to the sea below. Impulsively, she decided to keep walking. She needed to think and make some important decisions.

Maura didn't know how much longer she could stand living with Alec. She was sure he was having an affair with Zoe Allan. Not that that was the problem – it didn't even bother Maura that much. In fact, she was thinking about having one of her own. But Alec didn't know that!

Exercise 7: Verb forms. Lesen Sie weiter und setzen Sie die Verben im Simple Past ein!

pull   be   stop   look   want   remind

Maura **1.** _____ for a moment to look at the view. It **2.** _____ still very windy. The waves out at sea **3.** _____ all white and **choppy**. It was also cool and Maura **4.** _____ her fashionable raincoat more closely around her. It wasn't even a year old yet, but Maura **5.** _____ a new one. Alec had said no, she had to wait until next year. That **6.** _____ Maura about their fight late last night.

As usual, she and Alec had **argued** about money. Alec had once been a very rich man. That was one of the reasons Maura had married him only months after his first wife had died. The handsome shipbuilder with two little boys had been a very **good catch**. But in the last years, he had lost a lot of money. Business was down and expenses were up. Alec might even have to close down the shipyards. That wasn't public knowledge, though. Not even Jordan and Trent knew just how bad the financial situation was. Alec **was desperate for** money. He was even thinking about making some kind of deal with Ethan Saunders. She'd heard the two of them talk-

choppy	rau, bewegt
to argue	streiten
⚡ good catch	gute Partie
to be desperate for sth.	etw. dringend brauchen

ing several weeks ago at Alec's shipyards. It was something about "making a lot of money quickly if they put their heads together".

The sun was completely out now and it warmed her skin. Maura took off her raincoat. She was very near the edge of the cliff. The water below was **churning** and the waves sounded like thunder.

It's so wild and beautiful here, she thought.

That was almost the last thing she would ever think. Maura didn't see or hear the person who had come up behind her. No one else saw the hands that pushed her over the cliff. And no one except her murderer heard Maura's **terrified** scream as she began to fall. Her **arms flailed wildly** in the air as she tried desperately to find something to hold on to. Bizarrely, it looked as she were waving. But there was nothing except the water and the rocks. Maura was waving at death. Maura died **the instant** her head hit one of the rocks below. The cold waves washed over her lifeless body, but the rocks that had killed her kept it from being carried out to sea.

to churn	schäumen
terrified	angsterfüllt
to flail one's arms wildly	wild mit den Armen fuchteln
the instant	sobald

Exercise 8: Match-up. Ordnen Sie die Satzteile zu und unterstreichen Sie die richtige Variante!

1. ☐ Maura is / isn't   a) lots of money.

2. ☐ Alec needs / has   b) her murderer.

3. ☐ Alec might / will   c) having an affair.

4. ☐ Maura saw / didn't see   d) close down his business.

It was not the best weather for being out on the water, but Jordan and Phoebe were having a wonderful time. They had started the test run with the "Bee's Ghost" from the harbour at Yarmouth. This was the United Kingdom's smallest town and the location of the Bainbridge shipyards.

First, they had sailed around the Isle of Wight's most famous landmark. "The Needles" were a series of huge chalk rocks at the most western part of the island. Now they were more than halfway down the southern coast. Phoebe was paying careful attention to the **rugged** shore. There were all sorts of isolated places for smugglers to slip in and unload illegal drugs. The heavy winds would soon bring them past St. Catherine's Point and on to Ventnor and Monks Bays.

Those were the places that Director Sims had said were most important for Phoebe's investigation. She would have to find a way to get Jordan to slow down a bit. "Bee's Ghost" was simply fantastic in the water and the coastline was flying by.

rugged	schroff abfallend
to raise one's voice	die Stimme heben, lauter sprechen
ancestors *pl*	Vorfahren, Ahnen
to haunt	herumspuken in

"Jordan, why did you call her 'Bee's Ghost'?" Phoebe had to **raise her voice** so that Jordan could hear her over the wind.

"Oh, that's a long story. Did you know that the Isle of Wight is said to have more ghosts than any other island in the world?"

"Yes, of course! I've been away a long time, Jordan, but I'm still a caulkhead!"

Jordan laughed loudly. Phoebe had just spoken in the Isle of Wight dialect. "Caulkhead" meant someone who had been born to an old family on the island.

"Well, our manor house has a ghost, too. One of my **ancestors**, Beatrice Bainbridge, died mysteriously over 200 years ago. She's **haunted** the house and grounds ever since."

"What happened to her?"

Phoebe loved ghost stories.

"Well, no one knows for sure. Her body was found down on the rocks below the cliff. Some stories say she fell by accident, others that somebody pushed her."

"And how does she haunt the house?"

"Oh, the usual. We find doors open in the morning that were closed the night before. Candles go out suddenly for no reason. Sometimes, there are strange sounds in the middle of the night. Trent says ...," Jordan suddenly stopped talking.

He looked sad.

"What? What does Trent say?"

Jordan didn't know what else to say, so he told her the truth.

"Trent says that's why he started using drugs."

by accident	aus Versehen
to get in with a bad crowd	in schlechte Gesellschaft geraten
tense	angespannt

Phoebe's face showed how shocked she was.

"Oh, I don't believe him," Jordan continued. "That's just a stupid excuse. Trent got in with a bad crowd a few years ago. He's clean now, though. At least, that's what he's promised Dad."

"Oh, Jordan, I'm so sorry. Is that why things seem so tense between the two of them?"

"Well, it's part of it. Mainly, though, Dad thinks Trent should work harder. He was hoping the trip to South America would help Trent get more serious about the family business."

"And did it?"

"A little, I think. He was very excited about some of the contacts he made there. I hope he actually manages to sell some boats. The company could really use the money right now."

That was a good opportunity for Phoebe to ask Jordan how other shipbuilding businesses were doing. But just then, they started to sail past Ventnor.

Exercise 9: Tenses. Lesen Sie weiter und unterstreichen Sie die richtige Verbform!

"Oh Jordan, do you mind **1.** to slow / slowing down a bit? I'd love **2.** to try / trying and see Bainbridge Manor from the water."

"No problem, Phoebe. Whatever you want **3.** doing / to do . How about **4.** to sail / sailing up to the pier. I think I would enjoy **5.** to take / taking a little break."

"Oh, that's a great idea. I'd also like **6.** to go / going ashore."

Jordan slowed the yacht and Phoebe tried not to let her excitement show. It was news to her that the manor had a pier!
"And can you actually leave a bigger boat there overnight?"
"Sure. We often do a test run to here and the dock means we don't always have to sail back to Yarmouth the same day. That's really helpful, especially when a sudden storm comes up."
Phoebe was listening so carefully to Jordan's words that she almost forgot to watch the coastline. They were now moving at a much slower **pace**. She saw a little cove with a sandy beach, from which a **ravine** filled with trees led up to the cliffs. This place also wasn't that far from Ventnor.

ashore	an Land
pace	Geschwindigkeit
ravine	Schlucht

"Look, Phoebe!" Jordan was pointing to his right. "There's the roof of the manor."

Phoebe started to look in that direction. But her eyes spotted a bright red shape on the rocks. What could that be? She stared at it more closely. It looked like, like...

"Jordan, what's, what's that over there?" Phoebe's voice was starting to shake and she suddenly felt very cold.

Then Jordan saw it, too. The yacht was still too far away to be sure, but both of them were thinking the same thing. It looked as if they had just found a body.

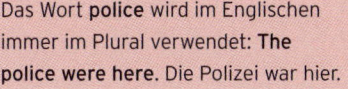
Das Wort **police** wird im Englischen immer im Plural verwendet: **The police were here.** Die Polizei war hier.

Jordan recovered from the shock first. He used the ship's radio to call the coastguard and police[i]. It was too dangerous to try and land the yacht directly on the shore. So Jordan brought the boat to the pier at Bainbridge Manor as quickly as he could. He and Phoebe secured it. Then they started walking carefully back along the rocky shore.

| to soak | durchnässen |
| wedged | eingekeilt |

The high waves soaked through their clothes. Phoebe slipped once and fell hard on one knee. Jordan took her hand and helped her back up. But he kept hold of her hand. They didn't speak the entire fifteen minutes it took to reach the spot on the shore where they had seen it. When they reached it, they saw that they had not made a mistake. The woman's body was wedged face down between the rocks. But they didn't need to see her face to know who it was. One hand had a bandage on it. And Phoebe and Jordan both recognized the dress. It was Maura's.

Phoebe shivered. She couldn't help remembering the story Jordan had told her about Beatrice. Bainbridge Manor might just have another ghost now. Maura certainly hadn't died easily.

Exercise 10: Crossword puzzle. Lösen Sie das Kreuzworträtsel!

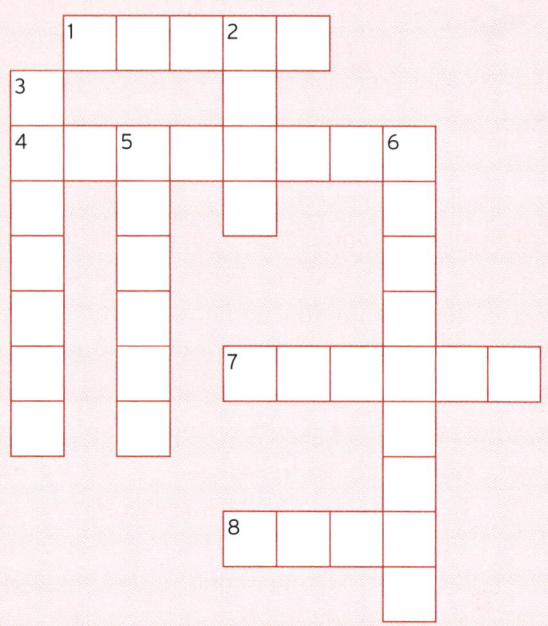

Across

1. Trent got in with a bad one.

4. Something you didn't plan or expect happens by...

7. a deep, narrow valley

8. another word for speed or tempo

Down

2. to force or squeeze something into a small space

3. A house that has a ghost is...

5. When the waves are wild and not calm, the sea is...

6. to be very, very scared

4. Waves of Suspense

"I'm certain it was an accident, Constable Quinn," Alec told the officer from the local police. "My wife must have slipped and fallen."

"Hm. Maybe. Still, I'm sure you understand that we have to investigate all the possibilities."

"Yes, of course, Constable. I know that. Let's **get on with it**."

Alec's eyes were red and he now looked much older than his 64 years. He had a glass of whisky in front of him, but wasn't drinking it. Alec, Jordan, Trent and Phoebe were all sitting in Alec's **study**. Constable Gregory Quinn and Inspector Malcolm Burrows from the Ventnor police station were questioning them. Maura's body had been **recovered** several hours ago. Now the police were trying to find out how – and why – she had died.

to get on with it	schnell weitermachen
study	Arbeitszimmer
to recover	*hier:* bergen

"So, who was the last person who saw her alive?" asked Burrows.

"I suppose that was me," answered Alec. "I went to her room around eleven last night to, um, say goodnight. She seemed fine."

Jordan looked at Alec strangely. He had heard his father and Maura arguing.

Phoebe saw the way Jordan was looking at Alec and she wondered what it meant. She would have to find out later, though, because Quinn was continuing with his questions.

Exercise 11: The definite article. Lesen Sie weiter und ergänzen Sie mit dem bestimmten Artikel „the", wo nötig!

"And none of you saw her leave 1. _____ house?"
"No, all of us left 2. _____ home very early in 3. _____ morning for 4. _____ work in Yarmouth. Maura always sleeps, I mean slept late. We thought she was still in 5. _____ bed," Trent answered 6. _____ question for all of them.

"And Maura was a drinker. Last night, she had a few too many."
"Trent! There's no need to tell the constables that." Alec was angry. "And you shouldn't **speak ill of the dead**."
"Calm down, Mr Bainbridge. We've already heard about your wife's, um, problem. And if she was, well, not quite **sober**, then she really could have fallen accidentally."
Burrows was about to continue his questioning, when the front doorbell rang. A few seconds later, Zoe Allan ran into the study.
"Alec, I'm so sorry. I came as soon as a heard. Can I..."
She stopped speaking when she saw the police officers.
"Oh, I didn't realize the police were here. I'll come another time."
"That won't be necessary, Ms Allan," Inspector Burrows replied. "Please take a seat. I understand you were also here last evening, so I will have some questions for you, too."

to speak ill of the dead	schlecht über Tote reden
sober	nüchtern

Zoe sat down in an armchair beneath the window that overlooked the drive. Inspector Burrows started to ask his next question. But he was interrupted again, this time by another constable coming into the room. He had a plastic **evidence** bag in his hand. Inside it was a light pink piece of paper.

"Inspector Burrows, have a look at this. We've just found this letter in Mrs Bainbridge's room. I think it's important."

Burrows took the paper and read it quickly to himself.

"Well, this **sheds a different light on** your wife's death, Mr Bainbridge. You didn't tell us that she was planning to **divorce** you. And you," Burrows was now pointing at Trent, "what exactly was going on between you and your stepmother?"

Alec and Trent both started talking at once. Burrows stood up and told them to be quiet.

"Let's do this one at a time, gentlemen. Mr Bainbridge senior, what was the true state of your marriage?"

"But Inspector, what does the letter say? Is it a **suicide note**?"

"Maybe, maybe not. Now answer my question, sir!"

Alec took a deep breath. He was starting to **perspire** heavily. "Our marriage was in trouble. But we were working on it."

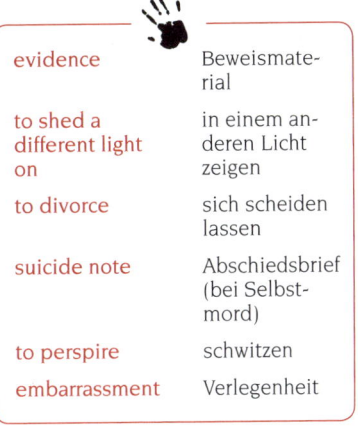

evidence	Beweismaterial
to shed a different light on	in einem anderen Licht zeigen
to divorce	sich scheiden lassen
suicide note	Abschiedsbrief (bei Selbstmord)
to perspire	schwitzen
embarrassment	Verlegenheit

"Well, it says here, 'My marriage to Alec is over. I don't know what to do. If I leave him, he will pay for his affair with Zoe Allan. But right now, he doesn't have any money.'"

Zoe's face was red with **embarrassment** when Burrows finished reading Maura's words. Jordan was staring at her in shock. But the others were looking at Alec.

"It seems you had a good motive for helping your wife over the cliff, sir. A divorce could have cost you everything."
"I loved my wife, Inspector. I have nothing else to say."
Alec's shoulders started shaking and a tear ran down his face.

to gasp	hörbar einatmen
outraged	empört
to swear	schwören
to demand	verlangen, fordern

"Fine. You can answer the rest of my questions later. I'll also need to speak with you, Ms Allan. But first, Trent Bainbridge, were you having an affair with your stepmother?"
Burrows' question made everyone in the room **gasp** in surprise.
"Certainly not! That is absurd." Trent tried to sound **outraged**. But he just looked scared. "Maura and I were close, of course. But there was nothing like that between us. I **swear** it."
"Well, explain this then," Inspector Burrows **demanded**, reading from the letter again. "'The situation with Trent is impossible – and dangerous. I must tell Alec. But the news will hurt him badly.'"
"I have no idea why she wrote that. Maura was an alcoholic. Who knows what crazy fantasies were going through her head."
"Trent, how could you?" Jordan shouted at his brother and jumped up from his chair.
Phoebe stood up quickly and put her hand on Jordan's shoulder. Her investigator's brain was

> Titel und Berufsbezeichnungen wie **Inspector** werden im Englischen nur groß geschrieben, wenn es sich um eine direkte Anrede handelt oder sie als Teil eines Namens verwendet werden, z. B. Inspector Burrows.

churning with thoughts. But her voice remained calm as she spoke. "Jordan, please sit back down and let Inspector Burrows do his job." Inspector Burrows gave everyone in the room a hard look. He decided not to read the last sentence of Maura's note out loud. It said 'Maybe I should just end it all.' That could mean that Maura Bainbridge had killed herself. He looked at his watch and sighed. This investigation was not going to be simple.

| to sigh | seufzen |
| foul play | *hier:* ein Verbrechen |

"It's late. I will have more questions for all of you tomorrow after the autopsy is finished. Maybe it will help us learn if Mrs Bainbridge's death was accidental, suicide or," he stopped for a second, "murder."

The way he said the last word made it clear that Inspector Burrows suspected foul play.

Exercise 12: Past tenses. Lesen Sie weiter und setzen Sie die Verben in die richtige Zeitform!

That's what Phoebe **1. think** _____, too. But she **2. not believe** _____ Maura **3. kill** _____ because of a possible divorce or affair. No one **4. notice** _____ Phoebe's surprise at the sight of Maura's letter. Phoebe **5. see** _____ that kind of pink paper before. It **6. look** _____ exactly like the stationery used by the writer of the anonymous tip about the smugglers!

Maybe Maura had known something and written to the Border Agency. And maybe someone had killed her to keep her from talking! And that someone was most likely a member of the Bainbridge family. It could even be Jordan!

Inspector Burrows and Constable Quinn were about to leave.

Burrows told everyone he would come back to Bainbridge Manor the next day around 11:00 a.m. He expected to find all of them waiting for him. Phoebe thought quickly. She had to find a way to speak to them alone and let them know that she was working undercover for the Border Force.

"Excuse me, I'll be right back. I need the, um, ladies room."

It was the best excuse she could think of. Phoebe left the room and tried not to look as if she were in a hurry. She caught up with the officers just as they were going out of the front door.

"Inspector, Constable, there's something important I need to tell you," Phoebe whispered.

She didn't want to take the chance that the others could **overhear** her.

"What is it, Ms Calloway?" Inspector Burrows asked.

He seemed **impatient** and in a hurry to **be on his way**. He and Quinn didn't stop, but kept moving out of the door and down the front steps.

Phoebe followed them to their car.

"Inspector, can we talk somewhere else? I have information..."

"Phoebe? What are you doing here?" Jordan had come out and was standing right behind her. "I thought you..."

to overhear	zufällig hören
impatient	ungeduldig
to be on one's way	auf dem Weg sein
to change one's mind	sich etw. anders überlegen

"Yes, Jordan, I know. I was just asking the officers if I really have to be here tomorrow. I had planned to do something else."

"But Ms Calloway, you said..."

Phoebe interrupted Inspector Burrows. "I've **changed my mind**, Inspector. Of course I'll be here."

Phoebe gave him a very meaningful look and hoped that he understood.
He did. "Well, actually, Ms Calloway, I don't have that many more questions for you. We could take care of them by phone. Here, take my card. You can call me in the morning."

Exercise 13: Synonyms. Welche Begriffe haben dieselbe Bedeutung wie die phrasal verbs? Ordnen Sie zu!

1. ☐ to find out   a) to return

2. ☐ to keep from   b) to discover

3. ☐ to come back to   c) to do

4. ☐ to take care of   d) to prevent

The Inspector wished Phoebe and Jordan a good evening. He and Constable Quinn went down the front steps and got in their police car. As soon as the car started down the drive, they began going over the facts in the case.
"Quinn, what do you think?"
"Well, Inspector, Maura Bainbridge's death

suspicious — verdächtig

looks **suspicious** to me. But what was all that with Ms Calloway?"
Inspector Burrows took out his mobile. "Oh, I think we won't have to wait long to find out. I expect Ms Calloway will call us the first chance she gets. Whatever it is she has to say, she certainly didn't want Jordan Bainbridge to hear it!"

Phoebe and Jordan watched the police car drive away. Then Jordan turned slowly towards Phoebe and looked at her curiously. She seemed nervous and was acting strangely. That business with the police officers just didn't **add up**.

to add up	*hier:* Sinn machen
to rush	schnell gehen, sich beeilen
ajar	angelehnt

"Phoebe, is everything okay?" he asked her and tried to take her hand. She wouldn't let him, though.

"I'm just upset, Jordan. Maura's death has shaken me. I think I need a few minutes by myself. If it's okay, I'll go up to my room."

"But Phoebe, I don't know if it's such a good idea for you to be alone right now. It's been a horrible day, for you, for all of us."

"Yes it has, Jordan. That's why I really do need to have a quiet moment or two. I won't be long. Then I'll come back downstairs. I think tonight, I could really use that brandy."

5. Catching the Waves

Phoebe **rushed** up the stairs to the guest room. She had an idea, but she would need to hurry.

Exercise 14: Prepositions. Lesen Sie weiter und fügen Sie die Präpositionen richtig ein!

on | to | inside | at | behind | out

She went **1.** _____ and made sure to leave the door **ajar** and not actually closed. Then she sat down **2.** _____ the dressing table. The mirror **3.** _____ it gave her a clear view of the door **4.** _____ her. Phoebe took **5.** _____ her phone and texted a quick message **6.** _____ Director Sims.

"Prepare for tomorrow night. Monk's Bay. Strange call coming. Inform Insp. Burrows, Ventnor police."

Phoebe added the number from the inspector's card to the message and hit the send key. Then she put down the phone and began brushing her hair and waiting. It didn't take long. Phoebe saw the door open just slightly. She was certain it was not the house ghost. No, a real live person was listening outside her door! Phoebe picked the phone back up and made a call.

"Hi Mum, it's me," she said as soon as someone answered at the other end. "No, things are not fine. Maura Bainbridge died today. No one knows for sure what happened. The police were here and the whole family is shattered. Me too. Oh Mum, it's all so awful."

Phoebe was crying now. She was a good actress and wanted to make sure her **red herring** worked.

"Yes, Mum," she said through her tears. "I'll try to calm down."

She paused for a moment. "Jordan? He's, well, he's **been a brick**."

"I need to go back downstairs now, Mum. I promised Jordan I'd join him for a drink. You too, Mum."

red herring	falsche Fährte
⚡ brick	prima Kumpel
to wait and see	abwarten und Tee trinken
helm	Steuer, Ruder
to down (a drink)	auf Ex trinken, runterkippen

As Phoebe said those words, she smiled to herself. The door was slowly closing again.

She lowered her voice. "It worked, Director Sims. Now we just have to **wait and see**."

Out on the open sea, the "Blues" moved up and down through the rough waves. Captain Rodriguez stood at the **helm**. He was still a little worried, but the ship should make it on time. He took another sip of his beer. Normally, he didn't drink on board. But he had just received a message from his contact on the Isle of Wight. It had said "Looking forward to seeing you." That was a code that meant everything was safe for the midnight rendezvous. Captain Rodriguez smiled broadly. With a little bit of luck, he could unload in just 24 hours. He **downed** the rest of his beer.

If all goes well, he thought, I can soon afford to drink champagne.

"In memory of my dear Maura," Alec said and raised his glass.
"To Maura," the others said and did the same.

Exercise 15: Was or were? Lesen Sie weiter und ergänzen Sie den Absatz mit **was** oder **were**!

The Bainbridge men, Phoebe and Zoe **1.** _____ all downstairs. Ethan Saunders **2.** _____ also there to **offer his condolences**. The atmosphere **3.** _____ sad and tense. They **4.** _____ all thinking about the woman who **5.** _____ no longer with them. Phoebe **6.** _____ watching them all carefully.

She still didn't know for sure which one of them had been **eavesdropping** at her door. Alec seemed **lost in thought**. Zoe kept trying to get him to look at her, but he just stared at the brandy in his glass. Jordan was very quiet. Every now and then, Phoebe saw him looking at her. Trent's eyes seemed strange and unfocused. Evan Saunders had asked several times about the police investigation.

to offer condolences	Beileid aussprechen
to eavesdrop	lauschen
to be lost in thought	in Gedanken versunken sein

"And the officers are coming back in the morning, I mean later today?" he asked.
It was already past midnight.
"Yes, Ethan. We've already told you that," Jordan said.

He put his glass down and stood up.

Ethan and Zoe realized they had outstayed their welcome. Both of them said again how sorry they were about Maura. Then they finally left the family alone with Phoebe. She too excused herself and went back upstairs. Alec and Jordan followed her a few minutes later. Trent remained in the study. When he was alone, he suddenly threw his glass against the wall.

"Oh Maura," he whispered.

The rest of his words remained unspoken. Trent was crying his heart out.

Early the next morning, Phoebe slipped out of the house. She had a long list of things to do. As soon as she had driven away from the house, she stopped to make some phone calls. The first one was to Inspector Burrows. He was already in the picture, so their conversation didn't take long. But now, she knew she could officially work with the local police. Next she phoned Director Sims at the Agency.

Her report to him took longer. After he had said yes to her plan, she drove inland to Newport, the

to outstay one's welcome	länger bleiben als es dem Gastgeber lieb ist
to cry one's heart out	sich die Augen ausweinen
to be in the picture	Bescheid wissen
Magistrate's Court	Amtsgericht
signed	unterschrieben
court order	Gerichtsbeschluss

main town on the island. There she went first to the Magistrate's Court to pick up a certain piece of paper. It was already signed and waiting for her. Director Sims had been quick to get the court order. Next, she went to a local bank, where the manager was already waiting for her. He didn't look happy when she showed him the court order, but he gave her the information she needed. It was very helpful. Phoebe was now sure that her suspicions were right.

Phoebe thanked the bank manager for his time and returned to her car. Now she just had to return to Bainbridge Manor and behave normally for the rest of the day. That night, Phoebe and the police were planning to catch the suspects red-handed.

Exercise 16: True or false? Welche Aussagen sind korrekt? Kreuzen Sie an!

1. Phoebe was certain that Jordan was the eavesdropper. ❏
2. Evan was curious about the police investigation. ❏
3. Trent cried many tears. ❏
4. Phoebe had to explain a lot to Inspector Burrows. ❏

The full moon was high in the night sky. But once again, dark clouds kept covering its light. Phoebe was dressed all in black, so no one could see her hiding on top of the cliffs. She raised infrared binoculars to her eyes.

She saw the outline of a large sailing ship out on the stormy sea. It had arrived a few minutes ago and its lights were off. She turned the binoculars towards the shore. There was the "Bee's Ghost" still anchored at the Bainbridge pier. A shadowy figure was moving towards it. Jordan. Phoebe sighed sadly. She hadn't wanted it to be him.

| to catch sb. red-handed | jmd. auf frischer Tat ertappen |
| binoculars *pl* | Fernglas |

A sudden movement on the water caught her attention. Another, smaller boat was getting closer to the larger ship. It had come from the other direction and also had no lights on. The waves were rocking it up and down. Phoebe saw the boat stop. She was not the only one watching. Someone on board threw out a rope. Another person on the bigger ship caught it and tied the two **vessels** together. It started to rain and the strong wind blew the drops into Phoebe's face. She ignored them. Suddenly, there was a lot of activity on board the two boats. The crew of the sailing ship began handing down boxes to the smaller boat. The two people on board took the boxes and put them below deck. Phoebe couldn't **make out** their faces. They were both wearing dark fisherman's caps and had their backs to her. It took quite some time to unload the boxes – there were so many of them. But finally, the transfer was finished. A tall man untied the smaller boat and immediately started to head for shore. But not towards the Bainbridge pier. The boat was going in the other direction! Phoebe looked quickly back towards the "Bee's Ghost." It was still there and so was Jordan. He was staring out at the water. There was no way he could see the boats, of course. Phoebe used her mobile to send a text message that said 'now'. Then everything began to happen at once.

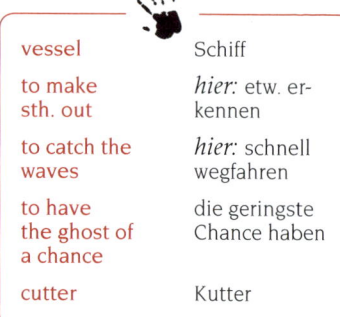

vessel	Schiff
to make sth. out	*hier:* etw. erkennen
to catch the waves	*hier:* schnell wegfahren
to have the ghost of a chance	die geringste Chance haben
cutter	Kutter

Four patrol boats raced out of the next cove where their captains had all just received Phoebe's message. Their spotlights lit up the Blues and the smaller boat. Both vessels tried to **catch the waves** and escape. But they didn't **have the ghost of a chance**. They were surrounded. Someone on board the smaller boat threw a box into the water. But one of the fast coastguard **cutters** was already right there. An officer recovered the box. Phoebe put down her binoculars. She didn't need them any more. The coastguard lights fell

handcuffs *pl*	Handschellen
time off for good behaviour	vorzeitige Entlassung wegen guter Führung
drug bust	Drogenrazzia
to waive one's rights	auf Rechte verzichten

brightly on the local smugglers. Zoe Allan and Ethan Saunders had been caught on the waves.

On board the "Blues," an officer put **handcuffs** on Captain Rodriquez. He was pretty sure there wouldn't be champagne in prison. And he could wave his fat bonus goodbye. The only thing he could hope for now was **time off for good behaviour**.

Phoebe and Jordan waved sadly at the ambulance and police car pulling away from Bainbridge Manor. It was late the next morning. So much had happened since midnight. On the two boats, the Border Force police had found more than 400 kilos of cocaine worth over 100 million pounds on the street. It was one of the biggest **drug busts** ever made in Britain.

Ethan Saunders was refusing to talk. But Zoe had **waived her rights** and told the police everything. Saunders' shipyard was almost bankrupt. Zoe's shipping company was in trouble, too. Phoebe had learnt that from looking at their bank records yesterday. That's why Zoe had gone into business with some of her "friends" in Columbia. She had con-

Wendungen mit **time:**	
for the time being	für den Moment
in time	pünktlich
time and (time) again	immer wieder
waste of time	Zeitverschwendung

vinced Ethan to use some of his smaller boats to smuggle the drugs into the rest of Britain. It still wasn't clear why Ethan had tried to involve Alec. But Alec had refused. He hated drugs and had secretly informed the Border Agency. The anonymous tip was from him. That was all shocking enough.

Exercise 17: Translation quiz. Übersetzen Sie und enträtseln Sie das Lösungswort!

1. seit _ _ _ □ _
2. schockierend _ _ □ _ _ _ _ _ _
3. überzeugen □ _ _ _ _ _ _ _
4. passieren _ □ _ _ _ _ _
5. Schiffswerft _ _ □ _ _ _ _
6. Mitternacht _ _ _ □ _ _ _ _
7. sich weigern _ □ _ _ _ _ _

Lösung: □ □ □ □ □ □ □

But then Inspector Burrows and Constable Quinn had come to arrest Trent. They had found him **unconscious** in his room and immediately called for the ambulance. Trent **was in a bad state**. He had taken an overdose of cocaine and left a suicide note. In it, he wrote that he had started taking drugs again and Maura had found out. She had **threatened** to tell his father. That's why he had killed Maura.

That news had been too much for Alec. He was inside now, downing a bottle of Scotch.

unconscious	bewusstlos
to be in a bad state	in schlechtem Zustand sein
to threaten	(be)drohen

"I wish you had trusted me, Phoebe." Jordan told her. "I can understand why you didn't, though. I was a suspect, too."

"I'm sorry, Jordan. I was just doing my job."

Phoebe looked at him and remembered that first kiss so long ago. She wished that she had time to stay and see what a second kiss would be like. But even though her investigation was over, Phoebe was still on duty. She had a report to write and had to return to London by the end of the day.

The next wave of crime was waiting…

Final Test

Answers

Glossary

List of Exercises

Final Test

Exercise 1: Match-up. Verbinden Sie die passenden Ausdrücke!

1. ☐ be up to   a) tears
2. ☐ an inside   b) no good
3. ☐ burst into   c) a grudge
4. ☐ hold   d) job

Exercise 2: Irregular verbs. Ergänzen Sie die fehlenden Verbformen!

	Infinitive	Present Participle	Simple Past
1.	_____	catching	_____
2.	_____	_____	told
3.	_____	losing	_____
4.	know	_____	_____
5.	_____	falling	_____

Exercise 3: Crossword puzzle. Lösen Sie das Kreuzworträtsel!

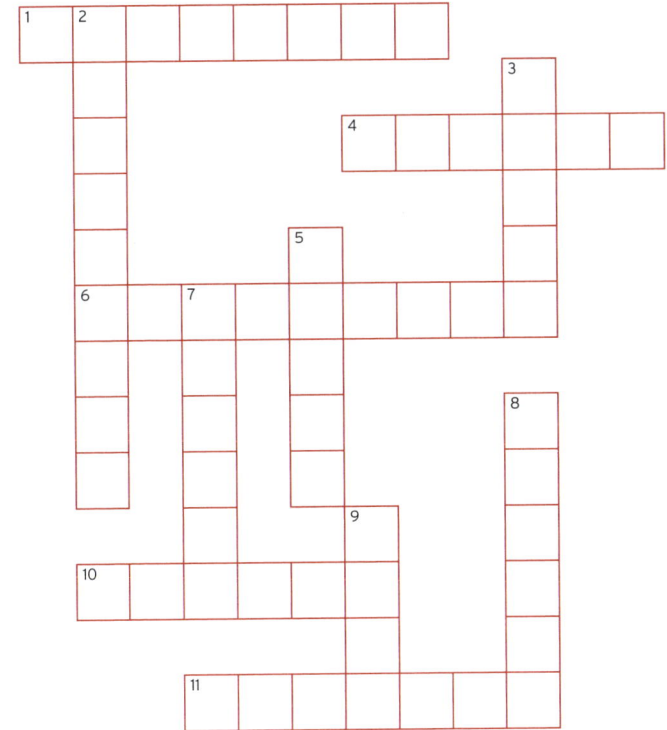

Across

1. older than a child but not an adult
4. a phone you can carry with you
6. an assistant who works in an office
10. a gentle wind
11. a small house

Down

2. very tired
3. not clean
5. unwanted plants
7. a dead body
8. plants and animals
9. a badger's home

Exercise 4: Translation. Übersetzen Sie folgende Sätze!

1. What am I going to do?

2. I saw that boy running from the woods.

3. The detective liked to visit the scene of the crime again.

4. We know you own a gun.

5. Did you recognize any of the men?

6. He turned and locked the door.

Exercise 5: Verb forms. Unterstreichen Sie die richtige Verbform!

1. Abigail always keep / keeps a fresh uniform in the office.

2. Brian is going / goes into retirement.

3. Dr. Liu Jing and Brian have known / are knowing each other a long time.

4. Abigail had done / was doing enough for one day.

5. Cooper wanted killing / to kill Cai, too.

Exercise 6: Plural forms. Bilden Sie die richtigen Pluralformen!

1. foot _____

2. person _____

3. man _____

4. Chinese _____

5. information _____

Exercise 7: What's wrong? Korrigieren Sie die folgenden Aussagen zu „The Spy's Last Shot", wo nötig!

1. Brian murdered Mr Chung because he was bribing Brian.

   _____

   _____

2. Tamsin O'Reilly was a computer expert for the City Council.

   _____

   _____

3. Abigail was an inspector and worked undercover for the police.

   _____

   _____

4. Cooper gambled a lot and offered Cai money for spying.

   _____

   _____

Exercise 8: Fill in the blanks. Ergänzen Sie die Redewendungen und enträtseln Sie das Lösungswort!

1. to call in ☐ _ _ _

2. to have enough on your ☐ _ _ _ _

3. to keep an _ ☐ _ on someone

4. the game ☐ _ up

5. to feel _ ☐ _ _ _ the weather

6. to ☐ _ back a long way

Lösung: ☐ ☐ ☐ ☐ ☐ ☐

Exercise 9: Verb forms. Vervollständigen Sie Phoebes Bericht an Direktor Sims!

"Last night, we **1. catch** _____ the smugglers red-handed. It **2. be** _____ one of the biggest drug busts ever **3. make** _____ in the UK! A. Bainbridge **4. give** _____ us the tip. Local police **5. arrest** _____ T. Bainbridge this morning. He **6. take** _____ cocaine again and M. Bainbridge **7. know** _____ it."

Exercise 10: Questions to the text. Fügen Sie das richtige Fragewort ein und beantworten Sie die Fragen zu „Waving Death"!

`what` `who` `when` `why` `how`

1. _____ did Maura die?

   _____

   _____

2. _____ made Phoebe suspect that Maura's death was not an accident?

   _____

   _____

3. _____ were the smugglers supposed to arrive?

   _____

4. _____ were Zoe and Ethan involved in drug smuggling?

   _____

   _____

5. _____ sent the anonymous letter to the Border Force and why did they do this?

   _____

   _____

Exercise 11: Unscramble the idioms. Ordnen Sie den Buchstabensalat, um die Redewendungen zu vervollständigen und enträtseln Sie das Lösungswort!

1. to have a lot on one's `dinm`   ☐ _ _ _

2. to get `cabk` on one's feet   _ ☐ _ _

3. to `epek` in touch   ☐ _ _ _

4. to mix business with `lesaprue`   _ _ ☐ _ _ _ _

5. to be `triwtne` in stone   ☐ _ _ _ _ _ _

6. the `oscta` is clear   _ _ ☐ _ _

7. to `vhae` a lot on one's mind   _ _ ☐ _

8. to put one's `dahes` together   ☐ _ _ _ _

9. to `kapse` ill of the dead   ☐ _ _ _ _

Lösung: ☐ ☐ ☐ ☐ ☐ ☐ ☐ ☐

Exercise 12: Multiple choice. Kreuzen Sie die richtige Variante an!

1. a) ☐ Phoebe grew up on the Isle of Wight.
   b) ☐ Phoebe has grown up on the Isle of Wight.
   c) ☐ Phoebe had growed up on the Isle of Wight.

2. a) ☐ Maura liked to sleep long.
   b) ☐ Maura was a long sleeper.
   c) ☐ Maura usually slept late.

3. a) ☐ Zoe said, "I hope we see us again."
   b) ☐ Zoe said, "I hope we see each other again."
   c) ☐ Zoe said, "I hope we meet us again."

4. a) ☐ Phoebe's boss has been the Director of the Border Force.
   b) ☐ Phoebe' chef was the Director of the Border Force.
   c) ☐ Phoebe's boss was the Director of the Border Force.

# Answers

Bullets over Bristol

Exercise 1: young, rested, full, thick, black, messy, relaxing

Exercise 2: 1. isolated 2. struggle 3. complain 4. undergrowth

Exercise 3: 1. Stephen's boots.
2. The caller's name.
3. Stephen's mother's voice.
4. The two constables' torches.
5. George Morris' family.

Exercise 4: 1. falsch 2. richtig 3. falsch 4. richtig

Exercise 5: 1. was listening 2. was holding 3. looked 4. felt 5. was 6. had introduced

Exercise 6: 1. exchanged 2. was 3. called 4. didn't 5. looked

Exercise 7: 1. a 2. b 3. b 4. a

Exercise 8: 1. hear 2. sympathetic 3. witness 4. calm

Exercise 9: 1. woods 2. silently 3. cottage 4. stepson 5. policeman 6. superior 7. shook
Lösung: witness

Exercise 10: 1. in 2. from 3. out 4. of 5. at 6. in

Exercise 11: 1. violent 2. stupid 3. sunrise 4. frantic 5. courage 6. impatience

Exercise 12: 1. stopped 2. went 3. shouted 4. came 5. demanded

Exercise 13: 1. The police arrested Stephen first.
2. Arthur told his wife he was going to hunt rabbits.
3. Arthur thought George owed him money.
4. Arthur's wife told the police he was not at home when George was murdered.

Exercise 14: 1. paler 2. close, closest 3. gentle, gentler 4. worse, worst 5. quiet, quietest 6. formal, most formal 7. more confident, most confident

Exercise 15: 1. gently 2. nervously 3. earnestly 4. miserably 5. comfortingly

Exercise 16: 1. c 2. d 3. a 4. b

Exercise 17: 1. went 2. didn't 3. leave 4. in 5. there 6. would 7. Did 8. who

The Spy's Last Shot

Exercise 1: 1. about 2. with 3. of 4. on 5. in 6. into

Exercise 2: 1. b 2. c 3. d 4. a

Exercise 3: 1. Who 2. Where 3. What 4. How

Exercise 4: 1. turned 2. thought 3. saw 4. was 5. started 6. was 7. were 8. was

Exercise 5: 1. false (She easily found a spot across the street from the pub.) 2. false (Brian had never used the message before.) 3. true 4. true

Exercise 6: 1. Chinese 2. had 3. outside 4. He'd 5. see 6. somebody/someone

Exercise 7: 1. had 2. was 3. wasn't 4. hadn't 5. had

Exercise 8: 1. d 2. c 3. b 4. a

Exercise 9: 1. thought 2. drank 3. had been 4. didn't have 5. needed

Exercise 10:

F	A	R	Q	L	W	O	T	N	X	I
I	N	V	E	S	T	I	G	A	T	E
N	D	I	Y	B	L	O	O	D	R	O
G	H	C	L	U	E	F	D	B	I	X
E	S	T	F	L	U	M	S	A	C	E
R	P	I	A	L	W	E	A	P	O	N
P	Y	M	J	E	I	Y	U	N	R	T
R	M	E	Z	T	T	O	T	W	O	K
I	B	A	R	S	N	T	O	Q	N	L
N	O	T	U	H	E	V	P	F	E	I
T	R	A	C	E	S	M	S	Y	R	S
S	G	C	T	L	S	I	Y	A	T	D

Exercise 11: 1. seriously 2. possible 3. secret 4. slightly 5. loudly 6. true

Exercise 12: 1. priority 2. offended 3. alternatives 4. trust

Exercise 13: 1. had 2. wasn't reading 3. was looking 4. was admiring 5. was running

Exercise 14: 1. tried 2. asked 3. wanted 4. said 5. rang 6. came

Exercise 15: **1.** c **2.** b **3.** d **4.** a

Exercise 16: **1.** He **2.** his **3.** him **4.** she **5.** himself **6.** her

Waving Death

Exercise 1: **1.** little **2.** such **3.** now **4.** lot **5.** When **6.** each

Exercise 2: **1.** man **2.** kind **3.** chef **4.** difficult

Exercise 3: **1.** gave, given **2.** went, gone **3.** found, found **4.** made, made

Exercise 4: **1.** perfect **2.** great **3.** closer **4.** interesting **5.** alone **6.** attractive

Exercise 5: **1.** everyone **2.** meet **3.** each other **4.** see **5.** us **6.** we

Exercise 6: **1.** Jordan said Phoebe's first evening back was really awful.
2. Phoebe told him she didn't want to have a nightcap.
3. Trent told Alec that Maura wanted to see him upstairs.
4. Alec wondered if the ghost of Bainbridge Manor was back again.

Exercise 7: **1.** stopped **2.** was **3.** looked **4.** pulled **5.** wanted **6.** reminded

Exercise 8: **1.** c, isn't **2.** a, needs **3.** d, will **4.** b, didn't see

Exercise 9: **1.** slowing **2.** to try **3.** to do **4.** sailing **5.** taking **6.** to go

Exercise 10:

Across: 1. CROWD 4. ACIDENT 7. RAVINE 8. PACE

Down: 2. WEDGE 3. HAUNTED 5. CHOPPY 6. TERRIFIED

Exercise 11: 1. the 2. – 3. the 4. – 5. – 6. the

Exercise 12: 1. was thinking 2. didn't believe 3. had been killed 4. had noticed 5. had seen 6. looked

Exercise 13: 1. b 2. d 3. a 4. c

Exercise 14: 1. inside 2. at 3. on 4. behind 5. out 6. to

Exercise 15: 1. were 2. was 3. was 4. were 5. was 6. was

Exercise 16: 1. false, Phoebe didn't know who had eavesdropped. 2. true 3. true 4. false, He was already in the picture.

Exercise 17: 1. since 2. shocking 3. convince 4. happen 5. shipyard 6. midnight 7. refuse
Lösung: cocaine

Final Test

Exercise 1: **1.** b **2.** d **3.** a **4.** c

Exercise 2: **1.** catch, caught **2.** tell, telling **3.** lose, lost **4.** knowing, knew **5.** fall, fell

Exercise 3:

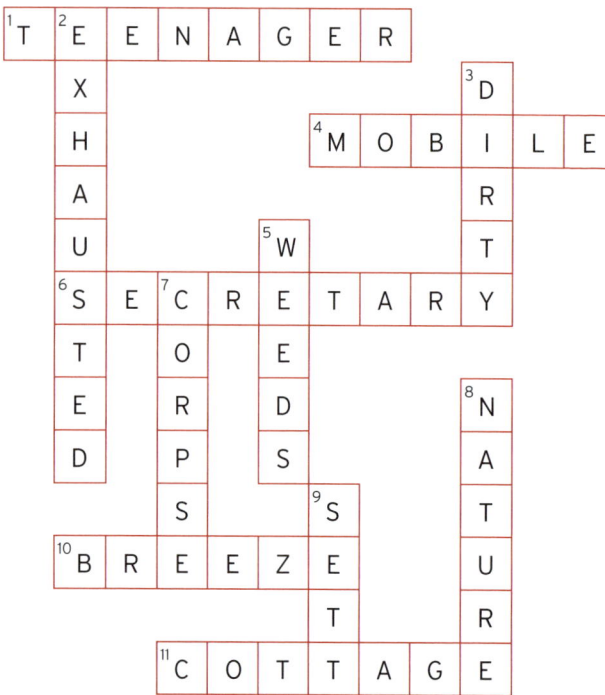

Exercise 4: **1.** Was soll ich nur machen?
2. Ich habe den Jungen aus dem Wald rennen sehen.
3. Der Detektiv ging gerne noch einmal an den Tatort zurück.
4. Wir wissen, dass du ein Gewehr besitzt.
5. Hast du einen der Männer erkannt?
6. Er drehte sich um und schloss die Tür ab.

Exercise 5: 1. keeps 2. is going 3. have known 4. had done 5. to kill

Exercise 6: 1. feet 2. people 3. men 4. (the) Chinese 5. information

Exercise 7: 1. Brian killed Chung in self defence because Chung was shooting at Brian.
2. Tamsin O'Reilly worked as an assistant to the Lord Mayor.
3. Abigail was a Superintendent and did not work undercover.
4. Cooper did not gamble a lot, he drank a lot. And it was Chung who threatened Cai that something bad would happen to her father if she didn't spy on her company.

Exercise 8: 1. sick 2. plate 3. eye 4. is 5. under 6. go
Lösung: spying

Exercise 9: 1. caught 2. was 3. made 4. gave 5. arrested 6. was taking 7. knew

Exercise 10: 1. How, Trent pushed her over the cliff and she hit her head on a rock and died instantly.
2. What, She recognized the light pink stationery.
3. When, At midnight on April 28th, two nights away.
4. Why, Both of their businesses were bankrupt / in financial trouble.
5. Who, Alec sent the letter because he hated drugs.

Exercise 11: 1. mind 2. back 3. keep 4. pleasure 5. written 6. coast 7. have 8. heads 9. speak
Lösung: make waves

Exercise 12: 1. a 2. c 3. b 4. c

Glossary

⚡ = umgangssprachlich
IRL = Irisch
pl = Plural

to accuse	beschuldigen
acquaintance	Bekanntschaft
to add up	*hier:* Sinn machen
agitated	aufgeregt
ajar	angelehnt
ancestors *pl*	Vorfahren, Ahnen
animatedly	angeregt
anxious	ängstlich
Area of Outstanding Beauty	Region von herausragender Schönheit, Naturpark
to argue	streiten
to arrest	festnehmen
ashore	an Land gehen
to assure sb. of sth.	jdm. etw. zusichern
at an angle	schief
at the mention	bei der Erwähnung

awful	schlimm, schrecklich
awkward	unangenehm, peinlich
⚡ Aye	Ja
to backfire	fehlzünden
back-up	Unterstützung
badger	Dachs
badger's sett	Dachsbau
barrel	Gewehrlauf
bay	Bucht
⚡ to be all over sth.	*hier:* sich über etw. hermachen
to be back on one's feet	wieder auf die Füße kommen
to be desperate for sth.	etw. dringend brauchen
to be in a bad state	in schlechtem Zustand sein
to be in the picture	Bescheid wissen
to be lost in thought	in Gedanken versunken sein
bent	gebeugt
to be offended	beleidigt sein
to be on call	Bereitschaftsdienst haben
to be on one's way	auf dem Weg sein
⚡ to be up to no good	nichts Gutes vorhaben
⚡ to be up to sth.	etw. vorhaben
to be written in stone	in Stein gemeißelt sein
to betray	betrügen
better safe than sorry	Vorsicht ist besser als Nachsicht
binoculars *pl*	Fernglas
to blackmail	erpressen

to blow sb.'s cover	jmd. enttarnen
to blush	erröten
booth	*hier:* Separee
bordering	angrenzend
to bow	sich verbeugen
breathless	atemlos
to bribe	bestechen
⚡ brick	prima Kumpel
bug	*hier:* Bazillus; Wanze
bully	Tyrann
to burst into tears	in Tränen ausbrechen
to buy some time	etw. Zeit gewinnen
by accident	zufällig
cabinet	Schrank
to call in sick	sich krank melden
to catch (caught, caught) sth.	*hier:* etw. verstehen, hören
to catch a glimpse	einen Blick erhaschen
to catch one's breath	*hier:* den Atem anhalten
to catch sb. red-handed	auf frischer Tat ertappen
to catch the waves	*hier:* schnell wegfahren
to change one's mind	sich etw. anders überlegen
cheat	Betrüger(in)
choppy	rau, bewegt
to churn	schäumen
City Hall	Rathaus
clearing	Lichtung
cliff	Klippe

clue	Hinweis
to combine business with pleasure	das Angenehme mit dem Nützlichen verbinden
comfortingly	tröstend
competition	*hier:* Konkurrenz
confident(ly)	selbstsicher
to confirm	bestätigen
confusion	Verwirrung
constable	Polizist(in)
content	Inhalt
coroner	Gerichtsmediziner(in)
court order	Gerichtsbeschluss
cove	Bucht
to crack	knacken
to crash	*hier:* brechen
to crawl	kriechen
creased	zerknittert
to creep	schleichen, kriechen
crime scene	Tatort
to cry one's heart out	sich die Augen ausweinen
curious	neugierig
to curse	fluchen
customs *pl*	Zoll
cutter	Kutter
to decipher	entschlüsseln
dead end	Sackgasse
to demand	verlangen, fordern
disbelief	Zweifel, Unglaube

to disturb	stören
to divorce	sich scheiden lassen
donation	Spende
⚡ to down drinks	Getränke hinunterkippen
downpour	Platzregen
downside	Nachteil
dreadfully	schrecklich
dressed up	aufgetakelt, schick angezogen
drug bust	Drogenrazzia
to dust for fingerprints	nach Fingerabdrücken untersuchen
earth bank	Erdhügel
to eavesdrop	lauschen
elderly	ältere(r, s)
embarrassment	Verlegenheit
evidence	Beweis, Beweismaterial
to explore	*hier:* durchsuchen
exterior	Außenseite
faint	schwach
fat cash bonus	fette Barprämie
⚡ to feel a bit under the weather	sich etw. angeschlagen fühlen
to fiddle	*hier:* herumspielen
fierce	wild, heftig
(to put) first things first	eins nach dem anderen (machen)
to fish for information	*hier:* nach Informationen suchen

⚡ fishy	suspekt, verdächtig
to flail one's arms wildly	wild mit den Armen fuchteln
flustered	aufgeregt
fool	Narr, Trottel
for ages	seit einer Ewigkeit
forensics	Kriminaltechnik
foul play	*hier:* ein Verbrechen
frantically	verzweifelt
frown	Stirnrunzeln
to frown	die Stirn runzeln
fur	Fell
gambling	Glücksspiel
gamekeeper	Wildhüter(in)
to gasp	hörbar einatmen, nach Luft schnappen
gasp of surprise	Laut des Erstaunens
gently	sanft, zärtlich
to get in with a bad crowd	in schlechte Gesellschaft geraten
to get on with it	schnell weitermachen
to get over sth.	mit etw. fertig werden, über etw. hinwegkommen
to get reacquainted with sb.	jmd. wieder besser kennenlernen
⚡ to get sth. over with	etw. hinter sich bringen
to glare at sb./sth.	etw./jmd. wütend anstarren
⚡ to go back a long way	sich schon lange kennen
⚡ to go on about sth.	sich über etw. auslassen
⚡ good catch	gute Partie

goods *pl*	Ware(n), Beute
to grab	greifen, schnappen
grand *IRL*	großartig
grateful	dankbar
groundsman	Platzwart
gun club	Schützenverein
half-shaved	halb rasiert
handcuffs *pl*	Handschellen
to haunt	herumspuken in
to have a lot on one's mind	den Kopf voll haben
⚡ to have a nerve	die Dreistigkeit besitzen
⚡ to have enough on one's plate	genug am Hals haben
to have the ghost of a chance	die geringste Chance haben
headquarters	*hier:* Präsidium
helm	Steuer, Ruder
hint	Hauch
to hiss	zischen
hold	*hier:* Frachtraum
to hold a grudge	einen Groll hegen
honoured	geehrt
hospitality	Gastfreundlichkeit
impatient	ungeduldig
indignant	empört
industrial espionage	Wirtschaftsspionage
injured	verletzt
in person	persönlich

⚡ inside job	Werk von Insidern
the instant	sobald
instantly	sofort
to interrupt	unterbrechen
interview room	Verhörraum
to investigate	untersuchen, ermitteln
investigation	Ermittlung
to keep in touch	in Kontakt bleiben
to keep one's side of the bargain	seinen Teil der Abmachung einhalten
lack of progress	mangelnder Fortschritt
⚡ lad	Junge
lame excuse	faule Ausrede
last orders	letzte Bestellung (vor Schließung des Pubs)
law enforcement force	Strafverfolgungsbehörde
leafy	mit viel Grün, belaubt
liar	Lügner(in)
line of business	Branche
literally	buchstäblich
lockers *pl*	Schließfächer
loner	Einzelgänger(in)
Lord Mayor	Oberbürgermeister
to lose one's temper	die Beherrschung verlieren
to lunge	losstürzen
ma'am	Abk. Madam, gnädige Frau
Magistrate's Court	Amtsgericht
magnificent	prachtvoll, großartig

mainland	Festland
to make a lot of waves	großen Aufruhr verursachen
to make sth. out	*hier:* erkennen
manor	Herrenhaus
mastermind	Drahtzieher, führender Kopf
meanwhile	währenddessen
memorial	Gedenkstätte
miserably	unglücklich
to motion to sb.	jmd. durch ein Zeichen auffordern
mousy	farblos
to mutter	grummeln
nightcap	Schlummertrunk
nightmare	Albtraum
to occur to sb.	jmd. einfallen
odd	ungewöhnlich, seltsam
to offer condolences	Beileid aussprechen
on tiptoes	auf Zehenspitzen
outraged	empört
to outstay one's welcome	länger bleiben als es dem Gastgeber lieb ist
to overhear (-heard, -heard)	zufällig hören
overweight	übergewichtig
pace	Geschwindigkeit
painkiller	Schmerzmittel
paperwork	Papierkram
passionate	leidenschaftlich
pasty	Pastete

patience	Geduld
patrol car	Streifenwagen
to perspire	schwitzen
pheasant	Fasan
pint	*hier:* Glas
politely	höflich
post mortem	Autopsie
to pound	hämmern
to pour	*hier:* fließen
to pretend	so tun als ob
property	Grundstück
to pull a pint	ein Bier zapfen
⚡ to pull oneself together	sich zusammenreißen
to pull the trigger	den Abzug betätigen, abdrücken
to punch in	eintippen
pursuer	Verfolger(in)
pushchair	Kinderwagen
to put a stop to sth.	einer Sache ein Ende machen
to raise one's voice	die Stimme heben, lauter sprechen
ramblings *pl*	Gefasel, Geschwafel
ravine	Schlucht
ray	Strahl
re:	AW: (E-Mail)
receiver	*hier:* Telefonhörer
recently	kürzlich
reception	Empfang

to recover	*hier:* bergen
red herring	falsche Fährte
regulars *pl*	Stammgäste
relentlessly	schonungslos
relief	Erleichterung
reluctantly	widerwillig
remarkable	auffallend, bemerkenswert
to remind sb.	jmd. erinnern
residue	Rest
retirement	Ruhestand
to reward	belohnen
robbery	Raub
to rock	schaukeln
rugged	schroff abfallend
to rush	schnell gehen, sich beeilen
rustling	Rascheln
to scan	*hier:* absuchen
self-defence	Selbstverteidigung
to shatter	(zer)stören, zerbrechen
shaving foam	Rasierschaum
to shed a different light on	in einem anderen Licht zeigen
shelter	Schutz, Unterschlupf
shifty	durchtrieben
shipwreck	Schiffsunglück
shipyard	Werft
shop talk	Fachsimpelei
shore	Küste

⚡ shot for the road	Absacker
shotgun blast	Schuss aus einer Flinte
to shrink (shrank, shrunk)	*hier:* kleiner werden
to shrug	die Schultern zucken
to sigh	seufzen
sigh of relief	Seufzer der Erleichterung
signed	unterschrieben
sinister	böse, unheimlich
to sip	nippen
sip	Schluck
Sláinte *IRL*	Prost (gälisch)
to slam	zuknallen
to slip	*hier:* hineinschleichen
to slip out	herausschlüpfen
smooth sailing	*hier:* ruhige Fahrt
to sneak out	sich herausschleichen
to snort	schnauben
to soak	durchnässen, durchsickern
sobbing	schluchzend
sober	nüchtern
solemnly	ernst
to speak ill of the dead	schlecht über Tote reden
to spill (spilt, spilt) sth.	etw. verschütten
splendid	großartig, prächtig, grandios
spooky	unheimlich
to spot sb.	jmd. sehen
spy	Spion(in)
stained-glass	Buntglas

stake-out	Observierung
to stammer	stottern
to stand out	sich abheben
standard operating procedure	übliches Vorgehen
stationery	Briefpapier
to steady	beruhigen
stern	ernst
strait	Meeresstraße
stubble	Bartstoppeln
study	Arbeitszimmer
to stumble	stolpern
suicide note	Abschiedsbrief (bei Selbstmord)
Superintendent	Hauptkommissar(in)
superior	Vorgesetzte(r)
support	Unterstützung
to surround	umzingeln
to survey	begutachten
suspect	Verdächtige(r)
suspension bridge	Hängebrücke
suspicious	verdächtig
to swear (swore, sworn)	schwören
sympathetically	mitfühlend
to tackle	angreifen
⚡ to take a long shot	etw. ergebnislos versuchen
to take in	aufnehmen; begreifen
tape recorder	Kassettenrekorder

target	Ziel
tea towel	Geschirrtuch
⚡ telly	Glotze
tense	angespannt
terrified	angsterfüllt
test run	Probelauf
the coast is clear	die Luft ist rein
the game is up	das Spiel ist aus
the Troubles *pl*	der Nordirlandkonflikt
to threaten	(be)drohen
threatening	bedrohlich
to thump	*hier:* pochen
time off for good behaviour	vorzeitige Entlassung wegen guter Führung
timidly	schüchtern
tipsy	beschwipst
torch	Taschenlampe
to trace	zurückverfolgen
traitor	Verräter(in)
to treat oneself to sth.	sich etw. gönnen
tremendous	enorm, gewaltig
to trespass	widerrechtlich betreten
⚡ troublemaker	Unruhestifter(in)
to trust	vertrauen
to turn up	auftauchen
twin city	Partnerstadt
unconscious	bewusstlos
undergrowth	Unterholz

unfortunate	*hier:* bedauernswert
United Kingdom Border Agency	brit. Grenzschutzorganisation
unsettled	unruhig
upsetting	verstörend
valuable	wertvoll
vessel	Schiff
victim	Opfer
wad	Bündel
to wait and see	abwarten und Tee trinken
to waive one's rights	auf Rechte verzichten
wedged	eingekeilt
weeds *pl*	Unkraut
weir	Wehr, Stauanlage
⚡ what's got into her	was ist mit ihr los
to whirl around	sich schnell drehen
wickedly	böse
to wink	zuzwinkern
witness	Zeuge, Zeugin
to yawn	gähnen

List of Exercises

Bullets over Bristol

	Focus	Exercise	Page
1	Grammar	Adjectives	7
2	Grammar	Unscramble	9
3	Grammar	Possessive apostrophes	11
4	Vocabulary	Right or wrong?	14
5	Grammar	Verb forms	16
6	Grammar	Fill in the blanks	18
7	Comprehension	Multiple choice	21
8	Vocabulary	Odd one out	23
9	Vocabulary	Fill in the blanks	25
10	Grammar	Prepositions	26
11	Vocabulary	Opposites	28
12	Grammar	Verb forms	30
13	Comprehension	Questions to the text	32
14	Grammar	Adjectives	34
15	Grammar	Adverbs	36
16	Vocabulary	Match up the words	37
17	Grammar	Choose the correct alternative	38

The Spy's Last Shot

	Focus	Exercise	Page
1	Grammar	Prepositions	43
2	Vocabulary	Synonyms	45
3	Comprehension	Questions	48
4	Grammar	Past tense verbs	50
5	Comprehension	True or false?	52
6	Grammar	Correct the mistakes	54
7	Grammar	Verb forms	56
8	Comprehension	Unscramble the text	58
9	Grammar	Tenses	60
10	Vocabulary	Hidden words	63

	Focus	Exercise	Page
11	Grammar	Adjective or adverb?	65
12	Vocabulary	Fill in the blanks	67
13	Grammar	Choose the correct alternative	69
14	Grammar	Verb forms	72
15	Vocabulary	Definitions	74
16	Grammar	Pronouns	76

Waving Death

	Focus	Exercise	Page
1	Grammar	Adverbs	82
2	Vocabulary	Odd one out	84
3	Grammar	Verb forms	86
4	Grammar	Adjectives	88
5	Vocabulary	Fill in the blanks	90
6	Grammar	Reported speech	94
7	Grammar	Verb forms	96
8	Vocabulary	Match-up	97
9	Grammar	Tenses	100
10	Vocabulary	Crossword puzzle	102
11	Grammar	The definite article	104
12	Grammar	Past tenses	107
13	Vocabulary	Synonyms	109
14	Grammar	Prepositions	111
15	Grammar	Was or were?	113
16	Comprehension	True or false?	115
17	Vocabulary	Translation quiz	118

Final Test

	Focus	Exercise	Page
1	Vocabulary	Match-up	122
2	Grammar	Irregular verbs	122
3	Vocabulary	Crossword puzzle	123
4	Grammar	Translation	124
5	Grammar	Verb forms	125
6	Grammar	Plural forms	125
7	Comprehension	What's wrong?	126
8	Vocabulary	Fill in the blanks	127
9	Grammar	Verb forms	127
10	Comprehension	Questions to the text	128
11	Vocabulary	Unscramble the idioms	129
12	Grammar	Multiple choice	130

Mit Sprachen glänzen –
SilverLine für Schule, Studium und Beruf

26 Reihen | 13 Sprachen | 205 Titel

SilverLine Lernbox • SilverLine Sprachkurs einfach & aktiv • SilverLine Wörterbücher
SilverLine Kochen auf … • SilverLine Typische Fehler • SilverLine Landeskunde
SilverLine Die 2000 wichtigsten Wörter • SilverLine Business English Trainer
SilverLine Bildwörterbuch • SilverLine Express • SilverLine Sprachrätsel
SilverLine Business Update • SilverLine … leicht gemacht • SilverLine Sofort sprechen
SilverLine Sprachführer für die Reise • SilverLine Update

Compact Verlag GmbH
Baierbrunner Str. 27 · 81379 München · Tel. 089/74 51 61-0 · Fax 089/75 60 95
www.compactverlag.de · www.lernkrimi.de

Compact Lernkrimi Classic

Compact Lernkrimis auch in Spanisch, Französisch, Italienisch, Deutsch und Schwedisch erhältlich.

A1

A2

B1

Art and Ashes
ISBN 978-3-8174-9493-4

Cook and Kill
ISBN 978-3-8174-9492-7

Crime Scene Tower of London
ISBN 978-3-8174-7687-9

Deadly Mistake
ISBN 978-3-8174-8259-7

Death Wasn't the Deal
ISBN 978-3-8174-9491-0

Der Rächer von Canterbury
ISBN 978-3-8174-7662-6

Der rote Nebel
ISBN 978-3-8174-7574-2

Ein fast perfekter Coup
ISBN 978-3-8174-7568-1

Game Over in Soho
ISBN 978-3-8174-7878-1

Hunting the Vampire
ISBN 978-3-8174-7305-2

Komplott unter Palmen
ISBN 978-3-8174-7571-1

Schüsse im Nebel
ISBN 978-3-8174-7763-0

The Mystery of the Mummy
ISBN 978-3-8174-7304-5

Tod eines Dandys
ISBN 978-3-8174-7660-2

Toxic Testament
ISBN 978-3-8174-7879-8

Sammelband 3 in 1 (B1/B2)

Inspector Hudson Investigates
ISBN 978-3-8174-7625-1

London Crime Time
ISBN 978-3-8174-7787-6

B2

Bloody Diamonds
ISBN 978-3-8174-9494-1

Das geheimnisvolle Gemälde
ISBN 978-3-8174-7306-9

Der Seelenjäger
ISBN 978-3-8174-7581-0

Der unheimliche Ritter
ISBN 978-3-8174-7661-9

Die Rache des Lords
ISBN 978-3-8174-7663-3

Die Spur des Höllenhundes
ISBN 978-3-8174-7307-6

Lady Mayfair's Revenge
ISBN 978-3-8174-7815-6

Nobody Dies Twice
ISBN 978-3-8174-9495-8

Schatten der Vergangenheit
ISBN 978-3-8174-7570-4

The Riddle of the Black Shoe
ISBN 978-3-8174-7638-1

Business English

Der 25-Millionen-Coup
ISBN 978-3-8174-7659-6

Teuflische Intrigen
ISBN 978-3-8174-7608-4

C1/C2

A Scottish Murder Mystery
ISBN 978-3-8174-8379-2

Compact Lernkrimi
Kurzkrimis

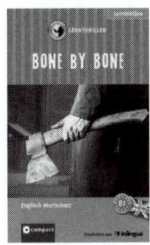

Compact Lernkrimi
Lernthriller

Death at Land's End ISBN 978-3-8174-9658-7 **The Murderer Next Door** ISBN 978-3-8174-9438-5		**A1**
Blood and Breakfast ISBN 978-3-8174-7760-9 **Deadly Business** ISBN 978-3-8174-9215-2 **It Was Murder, My Lord** ISBN 978-3-8174-7734-0 **Last Exit Waterloo Bridge** ISBN 978-3-8174-7733-3 **Murder at Teatime** ISBN 978-3-8174-7839-2 **Sammelband 10 in 1 (A2/B1)** **Murderous Collection** ISBN 978-3-8174-8967-1		**A2**
Bullets over Bristol ISBN 978-3-8174-8544-4 **Death Comes Knocking** ISBN 978-3-8174-7945-0 **American Business English** **Murderous Network** ISBN 978-3-8174-9312-8	**Bone by Bone** ISBN 978-3-8174-9497-2 **Massacre United** ISBN 978-3-8174-9319-7 **American English** **Faceless Killer** ISBN 978-3-8174-8856-8	**B1**
	In Terror ISBN 978-3-8174-8857-5	**B2**
		C1/C2

Compact Lernkrimi
Rätselblock

Compact Lernkrimi
Hörbuch

	Compact Lernkrimi Rätselblock	Compact Lernkrimi Hörbuch
A1	Murderous Games ISBN 978-3-8174-9500-9	
A2	The Art of Crime ISBN 978-3-8174-9155-1	A Shot in the Night ISBN 978-3-8174-8202-3 Death Wish ISBN 978-3-8174-8204-7 Strangled ISBN 978-3-8174-9665-5 The Butterworth Mystery ISBN 978-3-8174-8203-0
B1	A Deadly Puzzle ISBN 978-3-8174-8832-2	Bloody Revenge ISBN 978-3-8174-8860-5 Danger at King's Cross ISBN 978-3-8174-7673-2 The Thames Murderer ISBN 978-3-8174-7674-9
B2		Bloody Legacy ISBN 978-3-8174-7676-3 Die Intrigantin ISBN 978-3-8174-7675-6 **Business English** Crime & Company ISBN 978-3-8174-8976-3 Murder at the Office ISBN 978-3-8174-7747-0
C1/C2		

Compact Lernkrimi
Audio-Learning

Compact Lernkrimi
Sprachkurs

	Englisch für Anfänger (A1/A2) ISBN 978-3-8174-7784-5	**A1**
		A2
Totenstille im Hyde Park ISBN 978-3-8174-7797-5		**B1**
		B2
		C1/C2

Compact Lernkrimi
Spannend Sprachen lernen

Compact Lernkrimi Classic

> Spannende Krimistory mit über 70 Übungen
> Vokabel- und Infokästen direkt auf der Seite

ab 7,99 € (D)

Compact Lernkrimi Kurzkrimis

> Drei bzw. vier Kurzkrimis pro Band
> Ideal für den Einsatz an Schulen und VHS-Kursen

7,99 € (D)

Compact Lernkrimi Lernthriller

> Hochspannende Thriller mit Gänsehaut-Garantie
> 70 Übungen in ansteigendem Schwierigkeitsgrad
> Vokabel- und Infokästen

7,99 € (D)

Compact Lernkrimi Sammelband

> Drei Lernkrimis in einem Band mit über 300 Übungen
> Für mittleres bis fortgeschrittenes Sprachniveau

12,99 € (D)

Compact Lernkrimi Hörbuch

> Krimistory auf CD mit MP3-fähigen Tracks
> Begleitbuch zum Mitlesen inklusive Übungen und Vokabelangaben

9,99 € (D)

Compact Lernkrimi Audio-Learning

> Spannende Story im Buch
> Übungen zu Hörverständnis und Aussprache auf CD

9,99 € (D)

Compact Lernkrimi Sprachkurs

> Sprachen lernen für Anfänger
> Krimigeschichte in 10 Lektionen
> Vokabelkarten zum kostenlosen Download

14,99 € (D)

Compact Lernkrimi Rätselblock

> 10 Mini-Krimis mit 90 Rätselübungen
> Lösungen und Vokabelangaben auf der Rückseite
> Zahlreiche Illustrationen

5,99 € (D)

>> Jeder Band inklusive Abschlusstest und Glossar

Englisch | Spanisch | Italienisch | Französisch | DaF | Schwedisch

www.lernkrimi.de
www.compactverlag.de